Julius Caesar

By William Shakespeare

2

A Digireads.com Book
Digireads.com Publishing
16212 Riggs Rd
Stilwell, KS, 66085

Julius Caesar
By William Shakespeare
ISBN: 1-4209-2615-2

This book and many others are also available in electronic format.
Please visit *www.digireads.com* to purchase an ebook.

Dramatis Personae

JULIUS CAESAR, Roman statesman and general
OCTAVIUS, Triumvir after Caesar's death, later Augustus Caesar, first emperor of Rome
MARK ANTONY, general and friend of Caesar, a Triumvir after his death
LEPIDUS, third member of the Triumvirate
MARCUS BRUTUS, leader of the conspiracy against Caesar
CASSIUS, instigator of the conspiracy
CASCA, conspirator against Caesar
TREBONIUS, conspirator against Caesar
CAIUS LIGARIUS, conspirator against Caesar
DECIUS BRUTUS, conspirator against Caesar
METELLUS CIMBER, conspirator against Caesar
CINNA, conspirator against Caesar
CALPURNIA, wife of Caesar
PORTIA, wife of Brutus
CICERO, senator
PUBLIUS, senator
POPILLIUS LAENA, senator
FLAVIUS, tribune
MARELLUS, tribune
CATO, supporter of Brutus
LUCILLIUS, supporter of Brutus
TITINIUS, supporter of Brutus
MESSALA, supporter of Brutus
VOLUMNIUS, supporter of Brutus
ARTEMIDORUS, a teacher of rhetoric
CINNA, a poet
VARRUS, servant to Brutus
CLITUS, servant to Brutus
CLAUDIO, servant to Brutus
STRATO, servant to Brutus
LUCIUS, servant to Brutus
DARDANIUS, servant to Brutus
PINDARUS, servant to Cassius
The Ghost of Caesar
A Soothsayer, A Poet, Senators, A Cobbler, A Carpenter, Citizens, Soldiers, Commoners, Messengers, and Servants

ACT I

SCENE I. Rome. A street.

[Enter FLAVIUS, MARELLUS, and certain Commoners.]

FLAVIUS
Hence! home, you idle creatures get you home:
Is this a holiday? what! know you not,
Being mechanical, you ought not walk
Upon a labouring day without the sign
Of your profession? Speak, what trade art thou?

CARPENTER
Why, sir, a carpenter.

MARELLUS
Where is thy leather apron and thy rule?
What dost thou with thy best apparel on?
You, sir, what trade are you?

Second Commoner
Truly, sir, in respect of a fine workman, I am but,
as you would say, a cobbler.

MARELLUS
But what trade art thou? answer me directly.

COBBLER
A trade, sir, that, I hope, I may use with a safe conscience; which is, indeed,
sir, a mender of bad soles.

MARELLUS
What trade, thou knave? thou naughty knave, what trade?

COBBLER
Nay, I beseech you, sir, be not out with me: yet, if you be out, sir, I can
mend you.

MARELLUS
What meanest thou by that? mend me, thou saucy fellow!

COBBLER
Why, sir, cobble you.

FLAVIUS
Thou art a cobbler, art thou?

COBBLER

Truly, sir, all that I live by is with the awl: I meddle with no tradesman's matters, nor women's matters, but with awl. I am, indeed, sir, a surgeon to old shoes; when they are in great danger, I recover them. As proper men as ever trod upon neat's leather have gone upon my handiwork.

FLAVIUS

But wherefore art not in thy shop today?
Why dost thou lead these men about the streets?

COBBLER

Truly, sir, to wear out their shoes, to get myself into more work. But, indeed, sir, we make holiday, to see Caesar and to rejoice in his triumph.

MARELLUS

Wherefore rejoice? What conquest brings he home?
What tributaries follow him to Rome,
To grace in captive bonds his chariot-wheels?
You blocks, you stones, you worse than senseless things!
O you hard hearts, you cruel men of Rome,
Knew you not Pompey? Many a time and oft
Have you climb'd up to walls and battlements,
To towers and windows, yea, to chimney-tops,
Your infants in your arms, and there have sat
The livelong day, with patient expectation,
To see great Pompey pass the streets of Rome:
And when you saw his chariot but appear,
Have you not made an universal shout,
That Tiber trembled underneath her banks,
To hear the replication of your sounds
Made in her concave shores?
And do you now put on your best attire?
And do you now cull out a holiday?
And do you now strew flowers in his way
That comes in triumph over Pompey's blood? Be gone!
Run to your houses, fall upon your knees,
Pray to the gods to intermit the plague
That needs must light on this ingratitude.

FLAVIUS

Go, go, good countrymen, and, for this fault,
Assemble all the poor men of your sort;
Draw them to Tiber banks, and weep your tears
Into the channel, till the lowest stream
Do kiss the most exalted shores of all.

[Exeunt all the Commoners.]

See whether their basest metal be not moved;
They vanish tongue-tied in their guiltiness.
Go you down that way towards the Capitol;
This way will I disrobe the images,
If you do find them deck'd with ceremonies.

MARELLUS
May we do so?
You know it is the feast of Lupercal.

FLAVIUS
It is no matter; let no images
Be hung with Caesar's trophies. I'll about,
And drive away the vulgar from the streets:
So do you too, where you perceive them thick.
These growing feathers pluck'd from Caesar's wing
Will make him fly an ordinary pitch,
Who else would soar above the view of men
And keep us all in servile fearfulness.

[Exeunt.]

SCENE II. A public place.

[Music. Enter CAESAR; ANTONY, for the course; CALPURNIA, PORTIA, DECIUS
BRUTUS, CICERO, BRUTUS, CASSIUS, and CASCA; a great crowd following,
among them a Soothsayer.]

CAESAR
Calpurnia!

CASCA
Peace, ho! Caesar speaks.

[Music ceases.]

CAESAR
Calpurnia!

CALPURNIA
Here, my lord.

CAESAR
Stand you directly in Antonius's way,
When he doth run his course. Antonius!

ANTONY
>Caesar, my lord?

CAESAR
>Forget not, in your speed, Antonius,
>To touch Calpurnia; for our elders say,
>The barren, touched in this holy chase,
>Shake off their sterile curse.

ANTONY
>I shall remember:
>When Caesar says 'do this,' it is perform'd.

CAESAR
>Set on; and leave no ceremony out.

[Music.]

SOOTHSAYER
>Caesar!

CAESAR
>Ha! who calls?

CASCA
>Bid every noise be still: peace yet again!

[Music ceases.]

CAESAR
>Who is it in the press that calls on me?
>I hear a tongue, shriller than all the music,
>Cry 'Caesar!' Speak; Caesar is turn'd to hear.

SOOTHSAYER
>Beware the ides of March.

CAESAR
>What man is that?

BRUTUS
>A soothsayer bids you beware the ides of March.

CAESAR
>Set him before me; let me see his face.

CASSIUS
    Fellow, come from the throng; look upon Caesar.

[The SOOTHSAYER comes forward.]

CAESAR
    What say'st thou to me now? speak once again.

SOOTHSAYER
    Beware the ides of March.

CAESAR
    He is a dreamer; let us leave him: pass.

[Sennet. Exeunt all except BRUTUS and CASSIUS.]

CASSIUS
    Will you go see the order of the course?

BRUTUS
    Not I.

CASSIUS
    I pray you, do.

BRUTUS
    I am not gamesome: I do lack some part
    Of that quick spirit that is in Antony.
    Let me not hinder, Cassius, your desires;
    I'll leave you.

CASSIUS
    Brutus, I do observe you now of late:
    I have not from your eyes that gentleness
    And show of love as I was wont to have:
    You bear too stubborn and too strange a hand
    Over your friend that loves you.

BRUTUS
    Cassius,
    Be not deceived: if I have veil'd my look,
    I turn the trouble of my countenance
    Merely upon myself. Vexed I am
    Of late with passions of some difference,
    Conceptions only proper to myself,
    Which give some soil perhaps to my behaviors;
    But let not therefore my good friends be grieved—

Among which number, Cassius, be you one—
Nor construe any further my neglect,
Than that poor Brutus, with himself at war,
Forgets the shows of love to other men.

CASSIUS

Then, Brutus, I have much mistook your passion;
By means whereof this breast of mine hath buried
Thoughts of great value, worthy cogitations.
Tell me, good Brutus, can you see your face?

BRUTUS

No, Cassius; for the eye sees not itself,
But by reflection, by some other things.

CASSIUS

'Tis just:
And it is very much lamented, Brutus,
That you have no such mirrors as will turn
Your hidden worthiness into your eye,
That you might see your shadow. I have heard,
Where many of the best respect in Rome,
Except immortal Caesar, speaking of Brutus
And groaning underneath this age's yoke,
Have wish'd that noble Brutus had his eyes.

BRUTUS

Into what dangers would you lead me, Cassius,
That you would have me seek into myself
For that which is not in me?

CASSIUS

Therefore, good Brutus, be prepared to hear:
And since you know you cannot see yourself
So well as by reflection, I, your glass,
Will modestly discover to yourself
That of yourself which you yet know not of.
And be not jealous on me, gentle Brutus:
Were I a common laugher, or did use
To stale with ordinary oaths my love
To every new protester; if you know
That I do fawn on men and hug them hard
And after scandal them, or if you know
That I profess myself in banqueting
To all the rout, then hold me dangerous.

[Flourish, and shout.]

BRUTUS

What means this shouting? I do fear, the people
Choose Caesar for their king.

CASSIUS

Ay, do you fear it?
Then must I think you would not have it so.

BRUTUS

I would not, Cassius; yet I love him well.
But wherefore do you hold me here so long?
What is it that you would impart to me?
If it be aught toward the general good,
Set honour in one eye and death i' the other,
And I will look on both indifferently,
For let the gods so speed me as I love
The name of honour more than I fear death.

CASSIUS

I know that virtue to be in you, Brutus,
As well as I do know your outward favour.
Well, honour is the subject of my story.
I cannot tell what you and other men
Think of this life; but, for my single self,
I had as lief not be as live to be
In awe of such a thing as I myself.
I was born free as Caesar; so were you:
We both have fed as well, and we can both
Endure the winter's cold as well as he:
For once, upon a raw and gusty day,
The troubled Tiber chafing with her shores,
Caesar said to me 'Darest thou, Cassius, now
Leap in with me into this angry flood,
And swim to yonder point?' Upon the word,
Accoutred as I was, I plunged in
And bade him follow; so indeed he did.
The torrent roar'd, and we did buffet it
With lusty sinews, throwing it aside
And stemming it with hearts of controversy;
But ere we could arrive the point proposed,
Caesar cried 'Help me, Cassius, or I sink!'
I, as Aeneas, our great ancestor,
Did from the flames of Troy upon his shoulder
The old Anchises bear, so from the waves of Tiber
Did I the tired Caesar. And this man
Is now become a god, and Cassius is
A wretched creature and must bend his body,
If Caesar carelessly but nod on him.

He had a fever when he was in Spain,
And when the fit was on him, I did mark
How he did shake: 'tis true, this god did shake;
His coward lips did from their colour fly,
And that same eye whose bend doth awe the world
Did lose his lustre: I did hear him groan:
Ay, and that tongue of his that bade the Romans
Mark him and write his speeches in their books,
Alas, it cried 'Give me some drink, Titinius,'
As a sick girl. Ye gods, it doth amaze me
A man of such a feeble temper should
So get the start of the majestic world
And bear the palm alone.

[Shout. Flourish.]

BRUTUS
Another general shout!
I do believe that these applauses are
For some new honours that are heap'd on Caesar.

CASSIUS
Why, man, he doth bestride the narrow world
Like a Colossus, and we petty men
Walk under his huge legs and peep about
To find ourselves dishonourable graves.
Men at some time are masters of their fates:
The fault, dear Brutus, is not in our stars,
But in ourselves, that we are underlings.
Brutus and Caesar: what should be in that 'Caesar'?
Why should that name be sounded more than yours?
Write them together, yours is as fair a name;
Sound them, it doth become the mouth as well;
Weigh them, it is as heavy; conjure with 'em,
Brutus will start a spirit as soon as Caesar.
Now, in the names of all the gods at once,
Upon what meat doth this our Caesar feed,
That he is grown so great? Age, thou art shamed!
Rome, thou hast lost the breed of noble bloods!
When went there by an age, since the great flood,
But it was famed with more than with one man?
When could they say till now, that talk'd of Rome,
That her wide walls encompass'd but one man?
Now is it Rome indeed and room enough,
When there is in it but one only man.
O, you and I have heard our fathers say,
There was a Brutus once that would have brook'd
The eternal devil to keep his state in Rome

As easily as a king.

BRUTUS

That you do love me, I am nothing jealous;
What you would work me to, I have some aim:
How I have thought of this and of these times,
I shall recount hereafter; for this present,
I would not, so with love I might entreat you,
Be any further moved. What you have said
I will consider; what you have to say
I will with patience hear, and find a time
Both meet to hear and answer such high things.
Till then, my noble friend, chew upon this:
Brutus had rather be a villager
Than to repute himself a son of Rome
Under these hard conditions as this time
Is like to lay upon us.

CASSIUS

I am glad that my weak words
Have struck but thus much show of fire from Brutus.

BRUTUS

The games are done and Caesar is returning.

CASSIUS

As they pass by, pluck Casca by the sleeve;
And he will, after his sour fashion, tell you
What hath proceeded worthy note to-day.

[Re-enter CAESAR and his Train.]

BRUTUS

I will do so. But, look you, Cassius,
The angry spot doth glow on Caesar's brow,
And all the rest look like a chidden train:
Calpurnia's cheek is pale; and Cicero
Looks with such ferret and such fiery eyes
As we have seen him in the Capitol,
Being cross'd in conference by some senators.

CASSIUS

Casca will tell us what the matter is.

CAESAR

Antonius!

ANTONY
    Caesar?

CAESAR
    Let me have men about me that are fat;
    Sleek-headed men and such as sleep o' nights:
    Yond Cassius has a lean and hungry look;
    He thinks too much: such men are dangerous.

ANTONY
    Fear him not, Caesar; he's not dangerous;
    He is a noble Roman and well given.

CAESAR
    Would he were fatter! But I fear him not:
    Yet if my name were liable to fear,
    I do not know the man I should avoid
    So soon as that spare Cassius. He reads much;
    He is a great observer and he looks
    Quite through the deeds of men: he loves no plays,
    As thou dost, Antony; he hears no music;
    Seldom he smiles, and smiles in such a sort
    As if he mock'd himself and scorn'd his spirit
    That could be moved to smile at any thing.
    Such men as he be never at heart's ease
    Whiles they behold a greater than themselves,
    And therefore are they very dangerous.
    I rather tell thee what is to be fear'd
    Than what I fear; for always I am Caesar.
    Come on my right hand, for this ear is deaf,
    And tell me truly what thou think'st of him.

            [Sennet. Exeunt CAESAR and all his Train, but CASCA.]

CASCA
    You pull'd me by the cloak; would you speak with me?

BRUTUS
    Ay, Casca; tell us what hath chanced to-day,
    That Caesar looks so sad.

CASCA
    Why, you were with him, were you not?

BRUTUS
    I should not then ask Casca what had chanced.

CASCA

Why, there was a crown offered him: and being offered him, he put it by with the back of his hand, thus; and then the people fell a-shouting.

BRUTUS

What was the second noise for?

CASCA

Why, for that too.

CASSIUS

They shouted thrice: what was the last cry for?

CASCA

Why, for that too.

BRUTUS

Was the crown offered him thrice?

CASCA

Ay, marry, was't, and he put it by thrice, every time gentler than other, and at every putting-by mine honest neighbours shouted.

CASSIUS

Who offered him the crown?

CASCA

Why, Antony.

BRUTUS

Tell us the manner of it, gentle Casca.

CASCA

I can as well be hanged as tell the manner of it: it was mere foolery; I did not mark it. I saw Mark Antony offer him a crown;—yet 'twas not a crown neither, 'twas one of these coronets;—and, as I told you, he put it by once: but, for all that, to my thinking, he would fain have had it. Then he offered it to him again; then he put it by again: but, to my thinking, he was very loath to lay his fingers off it. And then he offered it the third time; he put it the third time by: and still as he refused it, the rabblement hooted and clapped their chapped hands and threw up their sweaty night-caps and uttered such a deal of stinking breath because Caesar refused the crown that it had almost choked Caesar; for he swooned and fell down at it: and for mine own part, I durst not laugh, for fear of opening my lips and receiving the bad air.

CASSIUS

But, soft, I pray you: what, did Caesar swoon?

CASCA

He fell down in the market-place, and foamed at mouth, and was speechless.

BRUTUS

'Tis very like: he hath the failing sickness.

CASSIUS

No, Caesar hath it not; but you and I,
And honest Casca, we have the falling sickness.

CASCA

I know not what you mean by that; but, I am sure, Caesar fell down. If the tag-rag people did not clap him and hiss him, according as he pleased and displeased them, as they use to do the players in the theatre, I am no true man.

BRUTUS

What said he when he came unto himself?

CASCA

Marry, before he fell down, when he perceived the common herd was glad he refused the crown, he plucked me ope his doublet and offered them his throat to cut. An I had been a man of any occupation, if I would not have taken him at a word, I would I might go to hell among the rogues. And so he fell. When he came to himself again, he said, If he had done or said any thing amiss, he desired their worships to think it was his infirmity. Three or four wenches, where I stood, cried 'Alas, good soul!' and forgave him with all their hearts: but there's no heed to be taken of them; if Caesar had stabbed their mothers, they would have done no less.

BRUTUS

And after that, he came, thus sad, away?

CASCA

Ay.

CASSIUS

Did Cicero say any thing?

CASCA

Ay, he spoke Greek.

CASSIUS

To what effect?

CASCA

Nay, an I tell you that, Ill ne'er look you i' the face again: but those that understood him smiled at one another and shook their heads; but, for mine own part, it was Greek to me. I could tell you more news too: Marellus and Flavius, for pulling scarves off Caesar's images, are put to silence. Fare you well. There was more foolery yet, if I could remember it.

CASSIUS

Will you sup with me to-night, Casca?

CASCA

No, I am promised forth.

CASSIUS

Will you dine with me to-morrow?

CASCA

Ay, if I be alive and your mind hold and your dinner worth the eating.

CASSIUS

Good: I will expect you.

CASCA

Do so. Farewell, both.

[Exit.]

BRUTUS

What a blunt fellow is this grown to be!
He was quick mettle when he went to school.

CASSIUS

So is he now in execution
Of any bold or noble enterprise,
However he puts on this tardy form.
This rudeness is a sauce to his good wit,
Which gives men stomach to digest his words
With better appetite.

BRUTUS

And so it is. For this time I will leave you:
To-morrow, if you please to speak with me,
I will come home to you; or, if you will,
Come home to me, and I will wait for you.

CASSIUS
I will do so: till then, think of the world.

[Exit BRUTUS.]

Well, Brutus, thou art noble; yet, I see,
Thy honourable metal may be wrought
From that it is disposed: therefore it is meet
That noble minds keep ever with their likes;
For who so firm that cannot be seduced?
Caesar doth bear me hard; but he loves Brutus:
If I were Brutus now and he were Cassius,
He should not humour me. I will this night,
In several hands, in at his windows throw,
As if they came from several citizens,
Writings all tending to the great opinion
That Rome holds of his name; wherein obscurely
Caesar's ambition shall be glanced at:
And after this let Caesar seat him sure;
For we will shake him, or worse days endure.

[Exit.]

SCENE III. The same. A street.

[Thunder and lightning.]

[Enter from opposite sides, CASCA, with his sword drawn, and CICERO.]

CICERO
Good even, Casca: brought you Caesar home?
Why are you breathless? and why stare you so?

CASCA
Are not you moved, when all the sway of earth
Shakes like a thing unfirm? O Cicero,
I have seen tempests, when the scolding winds
Have rived the knotty oaks, and I have seen
The ambitious ocean swell and rage and foam,
To be exalted with the threatening clouds:
But never till to-night, never till now,
Did I go through a tempest dropping fire.
Either there is a civil strife in heaven,
Or else the world, too saucy with the gods,
Incenses them to send destruction.

CICERO
Why, saw you any thing more wonderful?

CASCA
A common slave—you know him well by sight—
Held up his left hand, which did flame and burn
Like twenty torches join'd, and yet his hand,
Not sensible of fire, remain'd unscorch'd.
Besides—I ha' not since put up my sword—
Against the Capitol I met a lion,
Who glared upon me, and went surly by,
Without annoying me: and there were drawn
Upon a heap a hundred ghastly women,
Transformed with their fear; who swore they saw
Men all in fire walk up and down the streets.
And yesterday the bird of night did sit
Even at noon-day upon the market-place,
Hooting and shrieking. When these prodigies
Do so conjointly meet, let not men say
'These are their reasons; they are natural;'
For, I believe, they are portentous things
Unto the climate that they point upon.

CICERO
Indeed, it is a strange-disposed time:
But men may construe things after their fashion,
Clean from the purpose of the things themselves.
Come Caesar to the Capitol to-morrow?

CASCA
He doth; for he did bid Antonius
Send word to you he would be there to-morrow.

CICERO
Good night then, Casca: this disturbed sky
Is not to walk in.

CASCA
Farewell, Cicero.

[Exit CICERO.]

[Enter CASSIUS.]

CASSIUS
Who's there?

CASCA
A Roman.

CASSIUS
Casca, by your voice.

CASCA
Your ear is good. Cassius, what night is this!

CASSIUS
A very pleasing night to honest men.

CASCA
Who ever knew the heavens menace so?

CASSIUS
Those that have known the earth so full of faults.
For my part, I have walk'd about the streets,
Submitting me unto the perilous night,
And, thus unbraced, Casca, as you see,
Have bared my bosom to the thunder-stone;
And when the cross blue lightning seem'd to open
The breast of heaven, I did present myself
Even in the aim and very flash of it.

CASCA
But wherefore did you so much tempt the heavens?
It is the part of men to fear and tremble,
When the most mighty gods by tokens send
Such dreadful heralds to astonish us.

CASSIUS
You are dull, Casca, and those sparks of life
That should be in a Roman you do want,
Or else you use not. You look pale and gaze
And put on fear and cast yourself in wonder,
To see the strange impatience of the heavens:
But if you would consider the true cause
Why all these fires, why all these gliding ghosts,
Why birds and beasts from quality and kind,
Why old men fool and children calculate,
Why all these things change from their ordinance
Their natures and preformed faculties
To monstrous quality,—why, you shall find
That heaven hath infused them with these spirits,
To make them instruments of fear and warning
Unto some monstrous state.
Now could I, Casca, name to thee a man

Most like this dreadful night,
That thunders, lightens, opens graves, and roars
As doth the lion in the Capitol,
A man no mightier than thyself or me
In personal action, yet prodigious grown
And fearful, as these strange eruptions are.

CASCA
'Tis Caesar that you mean; is it not, Cassius?

CASSIUS
Let it be who it is: for Romans now
Have thews and limbs like to their ancestors;
But, woe the while! our fathers' minds are dead,
And we are govern'd with our mothers' spirits;
Our yoke and sufferance show us womanish.

CASCA
Indeed, they say the senators tomorrow
Mean to establish Caesar as a king;
And he shall wear his crown by sea and land,
In every place, save here in Italy.

CASSIUS [Drawing a dagger.]
I know where I will wear this dagger then;
Cassius from bondage will deliver Cassius:
Therein, ye gods, you make the weak most strong;
Therein, ye gods, you tyrants do defeat:
Nor stony tower, nor walls of beaten brass,
Nor airless dungeon, nor strong links of iron,
Can be retentive to the strength of spirit;
But life, being weary of these worldly bars,
Never lacks power to dismiss itself.
If I know this, know all the world besides,
That part of tyranny that I do bear
I can shake off at pleasure.

[Thunder still.]

CASCA
So can I:
So every bondman in his own hand bears
The power to cancel his captivity.

CASSIUS

    And why should Caesar be a tyrant then?
    Poor man! I know he would not be a wolf,
    But that he sees the Romans are but sheep:
    He were no lion, were not Romans hinds.
    Those that with haste will make a mighty fire
    Begin it with weak straws: what trash is Rome,
    What rubbish and what offal, when it serves
    For the base matter to illuminate
    So vile a thing as Caesar! But, O grief,
    Where hast thou led me? I perhaps speak this
    Before a willing bondman; then I know
    My answer must be made. But I am arm'd,
    And dangers are to me indifferent.

CASCA

    You speak to Casca, and to such a man
    That is no fleering tell-tale. Hold, my hand:
    Be factious for redress of all these griefs,
    And I will set this foot of mine as far
    As who goes farthest.

                [They join hands.]

CASSIUS

    There's a bargain made.
    Now know you, Casca, I have moved already
    Some certain of the noblest-minded Romans
    To undergo with me an enterprise
    Of honourable-dangerous consequence;
    And I do know, by this, they stay for me
    In Pompey's porch: for now, this fearful night,
    There is no stir or walking in the streets;
    And the complexion of the element
    In favour's like the work we have in hand,
    Most bloody, fiery, and most terrible.

CASCA

    Stand close awhile, for here comes one in haste.

CASSIUS

    'Tis Cinna; I do know him by his gait;
    He is a friend.

                [Enter CINNA.]

    Cinna, where haste you so?

CINNA

To find out you. Who's that? Metellus Cimber?

CASSIUS

No, it is Casca; one incorporate
To our attempts. Am I not stay'd for, Cinna?

CINNA

I am glad on 't. What a fearful night is this!
There's two or three of us have seen strange sights.

CASSIUS

Am I not stay'd for? tell me.

CINNA

Yes, you are.
O Cassius, if you could
But win the noble Brutus to our party—

CASSIUS

Be you content: good Cinna, take this paper,

[He gives CINNA the letter.]

And look you lay it in the praetor's chair,
Where Brutus may but find it; and throw this
In at his window; set this up with wax
Upon old Brutus' statue: all this done,
Repair to Pompey's porch, where you shall find us.
Is Decius Brutus and Trebonius there?

CINNA

All but Metellus Cimber; and he's gone
To seek you at your house. Well, I will hie,
And so bestow these papers as you bade me.

CASSIUS

That done, repair to Pompey's theatre.

[Exit CINNA.]

Come, Casca, you and I will yet ere day
See Brutus at his house: three parts of him
Is ours already, and the man entire
Upon the next encounter yields him ours.

CASCA
    O, he sits high in all the people's hearts:
    And that which would appear offence in us,
    His countenance, like richest alchemy,
    Will change to virtue and to worthiness.

CASSIUS
    Him and his worth and our great need of him
    You have right well conceited. Let us go,
    For it is after midnight; and ere day
    We will awake him and be sure of him.

[Exeunt.]

ACT II

SCENE I. Rome. BRUTUS's orchard.

[Enter BRUTUS.]

BRUTUS
    What, Lucius, ho!
    I cannot, by the progress of the stars,
    Give guess how near to day. Lucius, I say!
    I would it were my fault to sleep so soundly.
    When, Lucius, when? awake, I say! what, Lucius!

[Enter LUCIUS.]

LUCIUS
    Call'd you, my lord?

BRUTUS
    Get me a taper in my study, Lucius:
    When it is lighted, come and call me here.

LUCIUS
    I will, my lord.

[Exit.]

BRUTUS
    It must be by his death: and for my part,
    I know no personal cause to spurn at him,
    But for the general. He would be crown'd:
    How that might change his nature, there's the question.
    It is the bright day that brings forth the adder;
    And that craves wary walking. Crown him?—that;—
    And then, I grant, we put a sting in him,
    That at his will he may do danger with.
    The abuse of greatness is, when it disjoins
    Remorse from power: and, to speak truth of Caesar,
    I have not known when his affections sway'd
    More than his reason. But 'tis a common proof,
    That lowliness is young ambition's ladder,
    Whereto the climber-upward turns his face;
    But when he once attains the upmost round.
    He then unto the ladder turns his back,
    Looks in the clouds, scorning the base degrees
    By which he did ascend. So Caesar may.
    Then, lest he may, prevent. And, since the quarrel

Will bear no colour for the thing he is,
Fashion it thus; that what he is, augmented,
Would run to these and these extremities:
And therefore think him as a serpent's egg
Which, hatch'd, would, as his kind, grow mischievous,
And kill him in the shell.

[Re-enter LUCIUS.]

LUCIUS
The taper burneth in your closet, sir.
Searching the window for a flint, I found
This paper, thus seal'd up; and, I am sure,
It did not lie there when I went to bed.

[Gives him the letter.]

BRUTUS
Get you to bed again; it is not day.
Is not to-morrow, boy, the ides of March?

LUCIUS
I know not, sir.

BRUTUS
Look in the calendar, and bring me word.

LUCIUS
I will, sir.

[Exit.]

BRUTUS
The exhalations whizzing in the air
Give so much light that I may read by them.

[Opens the letter and reads.]

'Brutus, thou sleep'st: awake, and see thyself.
Shall Rome, & c. Speak, strike, redress!
Brutus, thou sleep'st: awake!'
Such instigations have been often dropp'd
Where I have took them up.
'Shall Rome, & c.' Thus must I piece it out:
Shall Rome stand under one man's awe? What, Rome?
My ancestors did from the streets of Rome
The Tarquin drive, when he was call'd a king.
'Speak, strike, redress!' Am I entreated

To speak and strike? O Rome, I make thee promise:
If the redress will follow, thou receivest
Thy full petition at the hand of Brutus!

[Re-enter LUCIUS.]

LUCIUS
Sir, March is wasted fourteen days.

[Knocking within.]

BRUTUS
'Tis good. Go to the gate; somebody knocks.

[Exit LUCIUS.]

Since Cassius first did whet me against Caesar,
I have not slept.
Between the acting of a dreadful thing
And the first motion, all the interim is
Like a phantasma, or a hideous dream:
The Genius and the mortal instruments
Are then in council; and the state of man,
Like to a little kingdom, suffers then
The nature of an insurrection.

[Re-enter LUCIUS.]

LUCIUS
Sir, 'tis your brother Cassius at the door,
Who doth desire to see you.

BRUTUS
Is he alone?

LUCIUS
No, sir, there are more with him.

BRUTUS
Do you know them?

LUCIUS
No, sir; their hats are pluck'd about their ears,
And half their faces buried in their cloaks,
That by no means I may discover them
By any mark of favour.

BRUTUS
    Let 'em enter.

[Exit LUCIUS.]

    They are the faction. O conspiracy,
    Shamest thou to show thy dangerous brow by night,
    When evils are most free? O, then by day
    Where wilt thou find a cavern dark enough
    To mask thy monstrous visage? Seek none, conspiracy;
    Hide it in smiles and affability:
    For if thou path, thy native semblance on,
    Not Erebus itself were dim enough
    To hide thee from prevention.

[Enter the conspirators, CASSIUS, CASCA, DECIUS BRUTUS, CINNA, METELLUS
CIMBER, and TREBONIUS.]

CASSIUS
    I think we are too bold upon your rest:
    Good morrow, Brutus; do we trouble you?

BRUTUS
    I have been up this hour, awake all night.
    Know I these men that come along with you?

CASSIUS
    Yes, every man of them, and no man here
    But honours you; and every one doth wish
    You had but that opinion of yourself
    Which every noble Roman bears of you.
    This is Trebonius.

BRUTUS
    He is welcome hither.

CASSIUS
    This, Decius Brutus.

BRUTUS
    He is welcome too.

CASSIUS
    This, Casca; this, Cinna; and this, Metellus Cimber.

BRUTUS
They are all welcome.
What watchful cares do interpose themselves
Betwixt your eyes and night?

CASSIUS
Shall I entreat a word?

[BRUTUS and CASSIUS whisper.]

DECIUS BRUTUS
Here lies the east: doth not the day break here?

CASCA
No.

CINNA
O, pardon, sir, it doth; and yon gray lines
That fret the clouds are messengers of day.

CASCA
You shall confess that you are both deceived.

[He points his sword.]

Here, as I point my sword, the sun arises,
Which is a great way growing on the south,
Weighing the youthful season of the year.
Some two months hence up higher toward the north
He first presents his fire; and the high east
Stands, as the Capitol, directly here.

[He points his sword.]

[BRUTUS and CASSIUS join the conspirators.]

BRUTUS
Give me your hands all over, one by one.

[Shakes their hands.]

CASSIUS
And let us swear our resolution.

BRUTUS

No, not an oath: if not the face of men,
The sufferance of our souls, the time's abuse,—
If these be motives weak, break off betimes,
And every man hence to his idle bed;
So let high-sighted tyranny range on,
Till each man drop by lottery. But if these,
As I am sure they do, bear fire enough
To kindle cowards and to steel with valour
The melting spirits of women, then, countrymen,
What need we any spur but our own cause,
To prick us to redress? what other bond
Than secret Romans, that have spoke the word,
And will not palter? and what other oath
Than honesty to honesty engaged,
That this shall be, or we will fall for it?
Swear priests and cowards and men cautelous,
Old feeble carrions and such suffering souls
That welcome wrongs; unto bad causes swear
Such creatures as men doubt; but do not stain
The even virtue of our enterprise,
Nor the insuppressive mettle of our spirits,
To think that or our cause or our performance
Did need an oath; when every drop of blood
That every Roman bears, and nobly bears,
Is guilty of a several bastardy,
If he do break the smallest particle
Of any promise that hath pass'd from him.

CASSIUS

But what of Cicero? shall we sound him?
I think he will stand very strong with us.

CASCA

Let us not leave him out.

CINNA

No, by no means.

METELLUS CIMBER

O, let us have him, for his silver hairs
Will purchase us a good opinion
And buy men's voices to commend our deeds:
It shall be said, his judgment ruled our hands;
Our youths and wildness shall no whit appear,
But all be buried in his gravity.

BRUTUS

O, name him not: let us not break with him;
For he will never follow any thing
That other men begin.

CASSIUS

Then leave him out.

CASCA

Indeed he is not fit.

DECIUS BRUTUS

Shall no man else be touch'd but only Caesar?

CASSIUS

Decius, well urged: I think it is not meet,
Mark Antony, so well beloved of Caesar,
Should outlive Caesar: we shall find of him
A shrewd contriver; and, you know, his means,
If he improve them, may well stretch so far
As to annoy us all: which to prevent,
Let Antony and Caesar fall together.

BRUTUS

Our course will seem too bloody, Caius Cassius,
To cut the head off and then hack the limbs,
Like wrath in death and envy afterwards;
For Antony is but a limb of Caesar:
Let us be sacrificers, but not butchers, Caius.
We all stand up against the spirit of Caesar;
And in the spirit of men there is no blood:
O, that we then could come by Caesar's spirit,
And not dismember Caesar! But, alas,
Caesar must bleed for it! And, gentle friends,
Let's kill him boldly, but not wrathfully;
Let's carve him as a dish fit for the gods,
Not hew him as a carcass fit for hounds:
And let our hearts, as subtle masters do,
Stir up their servants to an act of rage,
And after seem to chide 'em. This shall make
Our purpose necessary and not envious:
Which so appearing to the common eyes,
We shall be call'd purgers, not murderers.
And for Mark Antony, think not of him;
For he can do no more than Caesar's arm
When Caesar's head is off.

CASSIUS
    Yet I fear him;
    For in the ingrafted love he bears to Caesar—

BRUTUS
    Alas, good Cassius, do not think of him:
    If he love Caesar, all that he can do
    Is to himself, take thought and die for Caesar:
    And that were much he should; for he is given
    To sports, to wildness and much company.

TREBONIUS
    There is no fear in him; let him not die;
    For he will live, and laugh at this hereafter.

                    [Clock strikes.]

BRUTUS
    Peace! count the clock.

CASSIUS
    The clock hath stricken three.

TREBONIUS
    'Tis time to part.

CASSIUS
    But it is doubtful yet,
    Whether Caesar will come forth to-day, or no;
    For he is superstitious grown of late,
    Quite from the main opinion he held once
    Of fantasy, of dreams and ceremonies:
    It may be, these apparent prodigies,
    The unaccustom'd terror of this night,
    And the persuasion of his augurers,
    May hold him from the Capitol to-day.

DECIUS BRUTUS
    Never fear that: if he be so resolved,
    I can o'ersway him; for he loves to hear
    That unicorns may be betray'd with trees,
    And bears with glasses, elephants with holes,
    Lions with toils and men with flatterers;
    But when I tell him he hates flatterers,
    He says he does, being then most flattered.
    Let me work;
    For I can give his humour the true bent,

And I will bring him to the Capitol.

CASSIUS
Nay, we will all of us be there to fetch him.

BRUTUS
By the eighth hour: is that the uttermost?

CINNA
Be that the uttermost, and fail not then.

METELLUS CIMBER
Caius Ligarius doth bear Caesar hard,
Who rated him for speaking well of Pompey:
I wonder none of you have thought of him.

BRUTUS
Now, good Metellus, go along by him:
He loves me well, and I have given him reasons;
Send him but hither, and I'll fashion him.

CASSIUS
The morning comes upon 's: we'll leave you, Brutus.
And, friends, disperse yourselves; but all remember
What you have said, and show yourselves true Romans.

BRUTUS
Good gentlemen, look fresh and merrily;
Let not our looks put on our purposes,
But bear it as our Roman actors do,
With untired spirits and formal constancy:
And so good morrow to you every one.

[Exeunt all but BRUTUS.]

Boy! Lucius! Fast asleep? It is no matter;
Enjoy the honey-heavy dew of slumber:
Thou hast no figures nor no fantasies,
Which busy care draws in the brains of men;
Therefore thou sleep'st so sound.

[Enter PORTIA.]

PORTIA
Brutus, my lord!

BRUTUS

    Portia, what mean you? wherefore rise you now?
    It is not for your health thus to commit
    Your weak condition to the raw cold morning.

PORTIA

    Nor for yours neither. You've ungently, Brutus,
    Stole from my bed: and yesternight, at supper,
    You suddenly arose, and walk'd about,
    Musing and sighing, with your arms across,
    And when I ask'd you what the matter was,
    You stared upon me with ungentle looks;
    I urged you further; then you scratch'd your head,
    And too impatiently stamp'd with your foot;
    Yet I insisted, yet you answer'd not,
    But, with an angry wafture of your hand,
    Gave sign for me to leave you: so I did;
    Fearing to strengthen that impatience
    Which seem'd too much enkindled, and withal
    Hoping it was but an effect of humour,
    Which sometime hath his hour with every man.
    It will not let you eat, nor talk, nor sleep,
    And could it work so much upon your shape
    As it hath much prevail'd on your condition,
    I should not know you, Brutus. Dear my lord,
    Make me acquainted with your cause of grief.

BRUTUS

    I am not well in health, and that is all.

PORTIA

    Brutus is wise, and, were he not in health,
    He would embrace the means to come by it.

BRUTUS

    Why, so I do. Good Portia, go to bed.

PORTIA

    Is Brutus sick? and is it physical
    To walk unbraced and suck up the humours
    Of the dank morning? What, is Brutus sick,
    And will he steal out of his wholesome bed,
    To dare the vile contagion of the night
    And tempt the rheumy and unpurged air
    To add unto his sickness? No, my Brutus;
    You have some sick offence within your mind,
    Which, by the right and virtue of my place,

I ought to know of: [Kneeling.] and, upon my knees,
I charm you, by my once-commended beauty,
By all your vows of love and that great vow
Which did incorporate and make us one,
That you unfold to me, yourself, your half,
Why you are heavy, and what men to-night
Have had to resort to you: for here have been
Some six or seven, who did hide their faces
Even from darkness.

BRUTUS

    Kneel not, gentle Portia.

PORTIA

    I should not need, if you were gentle Brutus.
Within the bond of marriage, tell me, Brutus,
Is it excepted I should know no secrets
That appertain to you? Am I yourself
But, as it were, in sort or limitation,
To keep with you at meals, comfort your bed,
And talk to you sometimes? Dwell I but in the suburbs
Of your good pleasure? If it be no more,
Portia is Brutus' harlot, not his wife.

BRUTUS

    You are my true and honourable wife,
As dear to me as are the ruddy drops
That visit my sad heart

PORTIA

    If this were true, then should I know this secret.
I grant I am a woman; but withal
A woman that Lord Brutus took to wife:
I grant I am a woman; but withal
A woman well-reputed, Cato's daughter.
Think you I am no stronger than my sex,
Being so father'd and so husbanded?
Tell me your counsels, I will not disclose 'em:
I have made strong proof of my constancy,
Giving myself a voluntary wound
Here, in the thigh: can I bear that with patience.
And not my husband's secrets?

BRUTUS

    O ye gods,
Render me worthy of this noble wife!

[Knocking within.]

Hark, hark! one knocks: Portia, go in awhile;
And by and by thy bosom shall partake
The secrets of my heart.
All my engagements I will construe to thee,
All the charactery of my sad brows:
Leave me with haste.

[Exit PORTIA.]

Lucius, who's that knocks?

[Re-enter LUCIUS with LIGARIUS.]

LUCIUS
He is a sick man that would speak with you.

BRUTUS
Caius Ligarius, that Metellus spake of.
Boy, stand aside. Caius Ligarius! how?

[Exit LUCIUS.]

LIGARIUS
Vouchsafe good morrow from a feeble tongue.

BRUTUS
O, what a time have you chose out, brave Caius,
To wear a kerchief! Would you were not sick!

LIGARIUS
I am not sick, if Brutus have in hand
Any exploit worthy the name of honour.

BRUTUS
Such an exploit have I in hand, Ligarius,
Had you a healthful ear to hear of it.

LIGARIUS
By all the gods that Romans bow before,
I here discard my sickness!

[Pulls off his kerchief.]

Soul of Rome!
Brave son, derived from honourable loins!
Thou, like an exorcist, hast conjured up
My mortified spirit. Now bid me run,

And I will strive with things impossible;
Yea, get the better of them. What's to do?

BRUTUS
A piece of work that will make sick men whole.

LIGARIUS
But are not some whole that we must make sick?

BRUTUS
That must we also. What it is, my Caius,
I shall unfold to thee, as we are going
To whom it must be done.

LIGARIUS
Set on your foot,
And with a heart new-fired I follow you,
To do I know not what: but it sufficeth
That Brutus leads me on.

BRUTUS
Follow me, then.

[Exeunt.]

SCENE II. CAESAR'S house.

[Thunder and lightning.]

[Enter CAESAR, in his night-gown.]

CAESAR
Nor heaven nor earth have been at peace to-night:
Thrice hath Calpurnia in her sleep cried out,
'Help, ho! they murder Caesar!' Who's within?

[Enter a Servant.]

SERVANT
My lord?

CAESAR
Go bid the priests do present sacrifice
And bring me their opinions of success.

SERVANT
I will, my lord.

[Exit.]

[Enter CALPURNIA.]

CALPURNIA

What mean you, Caesar? think you to walk forth?
You shall not stir out of your house to-day.

CAESAR

Caesar shall forth: the things that threaten'd me
Ne'er look'd but on my back; when they shall see
The face of Caesar, they are vanished.

CALPURNIA

Caesar, I never stood on ceremonies,
Yet now they fright me. There is one within,
Besides the things that we have heard and seen,
Recounts most horrid sights seen by the watch.
A lioness hath whelped in the streets;
And graves have yawn'd, and yielded up their dead;
Fierce fiery warriors fought upon the clouds,
In ranks and squadrons and right form of war,
Which drizzled blood upon the Capitol;
The noise of battle hurtled in the air,
Horses did neigh, and dying men did groan,
And ghosts did shriek and squeal about the streets.
O Caesar! these things are beyond all use,
And I do fear them.

CAESAR

What can be avoided
Whose end is purposed by the mighty gods?
Yet Caesar shall go forth; for these predictions
Are to the world in general as to Caesar.

CALPURNIA

When beggars die, there are no comets seen;
The heavens themselves blaze forth the death of princes.

CAESAR

Cowards die many times before their deaths;
The valiant never taste of death but once.
Of all the wonders that I yet have heard.
It seems to me most strange that men should fear;
Seeing that death, a necessary end,
Will come when it will come.

[Re-enter Servant.]

What say the augurers?

SERVANT
    They would not have you to stir forth to-day.
    Plucking the entrails of an offering forth,
    They could not find a heart within the beast.

CAESAR
    The gods do this in shame of cowardice:
    Caesar should be a beast without a heart,
    If he should stay at home to-day for fear.
    No, Caesar shall not: danger knows full well
    That Caesar is more dangerous than he:
    We are two lions litter'd in one day,
    And I the elder and more terrible:
    And Caesar shall go forth.

CALPURNIA
    Alas, my lord,
    Your wisdom is consumed in confidence.
    Do not go forth to-day: call it my fear
    That keeps you in the house, and not your own.
    We'll send Mark Antony to the senate-house:
    And he shall say you are not well to-day:
    Let me, upon my knee, prevail in this.

[CALPURNIA kneels]

CAESAR
    Mark Antony shall say I am not well,
    And, for thy humour, I will stay at home.

[Enter DECIUS BRUTUS.]

Here's Decius Brutus, he shall tell them so.

[CALPURNIA rises.]

DECIUS BRUTUS
    Caesar, all hail! good morrow, worthy Caesar:
    I come to fetch you to the senate-house.

CAESAR

> And you are come in very happy time,
> To bear my greeting to the senators
> And tell them that I will not come to-day:
> Cannot, is false, and that I dare not, falser:
> I will not come to-day: tell them so, Decius.

CALPURNIA

> Say he is sick.

CAESAR

> Shall Caesar send a lie?
> Have I in conquest stretch'd mine arm so far,
> To be afraid to tell graybeards the truth?
> Decius, go tell them Caesar will not come.

DECIUS BRUTUS

> Most mighty Caesar, let me know some cause,
> Lest I be laugh'd at when I tell them so.

CAESAR

> The cause is in my will: I will not come;
> That is enough to satisfy the senate.
> But for your private satisfaction,
> Because I love you, I will let you know:
> Calpurnia here, my wife, stays me at home:
> She dreamt to-night she saw my statue,
> Which, like a fountain with an hundred spouts,
> Did run pure blood: and many lusty Romans
> Came smiling, and did bathe their hands in it:
> And these does she apply for warnings, and portents,
> And evils imminent; and on her knee
> Hath begg'd that I will stay at home to-day.

DECIUS BRUTUS

> This dream is all amiss interpreted;
> It was a vision fair and fortunate:
> Your statue spouting blood in many pipes,
> In which so many smiling Romans bathed,
> Signifies that from you great Rome shall suck
> Reviving blood, and that great men shall press
> For tinctures, stains, relics and cognizance.
> This by Calpurnia's dream is signified.

CAESAR

> And this way have you well expounded it.

DECIUS BRUTUS
    I have, when you have heard what I can say:
    And know it now: the senate have concluded
    To give this day a crown to mighty Caesar.
    If you shall send them word you will not come,
    Their minds may change. Besides, it were a mock
    Apt to be render'd, for some one to say
    'Break up the senate till another time,
    When Caesar's wife shall meet with better dreams.'
    If Caesar hide himself, shall they not whisper
    'Lo, Caesar is afraid'?
    Pardon me, Caesar; for my dear dear love
    To our proceeding bids me tell you this;
    And reason to my love is liable.

CAESAR
    How foolish do your fears seem now, Calpurnia!
    I am ashamed I did yield to them.
    Give me my robe, for I will go.

[Enter PUBLIUS, BRUTUS, LIGARIUS, METELLUS, CASCA, TREBONIUS, and
CINNA.]

    And look where Publius is come to fetch me.

PUBLIUS
    Good morrow, Caesar.

CAESAR
    Welcome, Publius.
    What, Brutus, are you stirr'd so early too?
    Good morrow, Casca. Caius Ligarius,
    Caesar was ne'er so much your enemy
    As that same ague which hath made you lean.
    What is 't o'clock?

BRUTUS
    Caesar, 'tis strucken eight.

CAESAR
    I thank you for your pains and courtesy.

[Enter ANTONY.]

    See! Antony, that revels long o' nights,
    Is notwithstanding up. Good morrow, Antony.

ANTONY
      So to most noble Caesar.

CAESAR [To CALPURNIA.]
      Bid them prepare within:
      I am to blame to be thus waited for.

                    [Exit CALPURNIA.]

      Now, Cinna: now, Metellus: what, Trebonius!
      I have an hour's talk in store for you;
      Remember that you call on me to-day:
      Be near me, that I may remember you.

TREBONIUS
      Caesar, I will: [Aside.] and so near will I be,
      That your best friends shall wish I had been further.

CAESAR
      Good friends, go in, and taste some wine with me;
      And we, like friends, will straightway go together.

BRUTUS [Aside]
      That every like is not the same, O Caesar,
      The heart of Brutus yearns to think upon!

                    [Exeunt.]

           SCENE III. A street near the Capitol.

        [Enter ARTEMIDORUS, reading a paper.]

ARTEMIDORUS
      'Caesar, beware of Brutus; take heed of Cassius; come not near Casca; have
      an eye to Cinna, trust not Trebonius: mark well Metellus Cimber: Decius
      Brutus loves thee not: thou hast wronged Caius Ligarius. There is but one
      mind in all these men, and it is bent against Caesar. If thou beest not
      immortal, look about you: security gives way to conspiracy. The mighty
      gods defend thee! Thy lover, 'ARTEMIDORUS.'

      Here will I stand till Caesar pass along,
      And as a suitor will I give him this.
      My heart laments that virtue cannot live
      Out of the teeth of emulation.
      If thou read this, O Caesar, thou mayst live;
      If not, the Fates with traitors do contrive.

[Exit.]

SCENE IV. Another part of the same street, before the house of BRUTUS.

[Enter PORTIA and LUCIUS.]

PORTIA
I prithee, boy, run to the senate-house;
Stay not to answer me, but get thee gone:
Why dost thou stay?

LUCIUS
To know my errand, madam.

PORTIA
I would have had thee there, and here again,
Ere I can tell thee what thou shouldst do there.
O constancy, be strong upon my side,
Set a huge mountain 'tween my heart and tongue!
I have a man's mind, but a woman's might.
How hard it is for women to keep counsel!
Art thou here yet?

LUCIUS
Madam, what should I do?
Run to the Capitol, and nothing else?
And so return to you, and nothing else?

PORTIA
Yes, bring me word, boy, if thy lord look well,
For he went sickly forth: and take good note
What Caesar doth, what suitors press to him.
Hark, boy! what noise is that?

LUCIUS
I hear none, madam.

PORTIA
Prithee, listen well;
I heard a bustling rumour, like a fray,
And the wind brings it from the Capitol.

LUCIUS
Sooth, madam, I hear nothing.

[Enter the Soothsayer.]

PORTIA
Come hither, fellow: which way hast thou been?

SOOTHSAYER
At mine own house, good lady.

PORTIA
What is't o'clock?

SOOTHSAYER
About the ninth hour, lady.

PORTIA
Is Caesar yet gone to the Capitol?

SOOTHSAYER
Madam, not yet: I go to take my stand,
To see him pass on to the Capitol.

PORTIA
Thou hast some suit to Caesar, hast thou not?

SOOTHSAYER
That I have, lady: if it will please Caesar
To be so good to Caesar as to hear me,
I shall beseech him to befriend himself.

PORTIA
Why, know'st thou any harm's intended towards him?

SOOTHSAYER
None that I know will be, much that I fear may chance.
Good morrow to you. [Moves away.]
Here the street is narrow:
The throng that follows Caesar at the heels,
Of senators, of praetors, common suitors,
Will crowd a feeble man almost to death:
I'll get me to a place more void, and there
Speak to great Caesar as he comes along.

[Exit.]

PORTIA [Aside.]
    I must go in. Ay me, how weak a thing
    The heart of woman is! O Brutus,
    The heavens speed thee in thine enterprise!
    Sure, the boy heard me: [To LUCIUS.] Brutus hath a suit
    That Caesar will not grant. [Aside.] O, I grow faint.
    [To LUCIUS.] Run, Lucius, and commend me to my lord;
    Say I am merry: come to me again,
    And bring me word what he doth say to thee.

[Exeunt severally.]

ACT III

SCENE I. Rome. Before the Capitol; the Senate sitting above.

[A crowd of people; among them ARTEMIDORUS and the Soothsayer. Flourish. Enter CAESAR, BRUTUS, CASSIUS, CASCA, DECIUS BRUTUS, METELLUS CIMBER, TREBONIUS, CINNA, ANTONY, LEPIDUS, POPILLIUS, PUBLIUS, and others.]

CAESAR
    [To the SOOTHSAYER.] The ides of March are come.

SOOTHSAYER
    Ay, Caesar; but not gone.

ARTEMIDORUS
    Hail, Caesar! Read this schedule.

DECIUS BRUTUS
    Trebonius doth desire you to o'erread,
    At your best leisure, this his humble suit.

ARTEMIDORUS
    O Caesar, read mine first; for mine's a suit
    That touches Caesar nearer: read it, great Caesar.

CAESAR
    What touches us ourself shall be last served.

ARTEMIDORUS
    Delay not, Caesar; read it instantly.

CAESAR
    What, is the fellow mad?

PUBLIUS [To ARTEMIDORUS.]
Sirrah, give place.

CASSIUS [To ARTEMIDORUS.]
What, urge you your petitions in the street?
Come to the Capitol.

[CAESAR goes up to the Senate-House, the rest following.]

POPILLIUS
I wish your enterprise to-day may thrive.

CASSIUS
What enterprise, Popillius?

POPILLIUS
Fare you well.

[Advances to CAESAR.]

BRUTUS
What said Popillius Lena?

CASSIUS
He wish'd to-day our enterprise might thrive.
I fear our purpose is discovered.

BRUTUS
Look, how he makes to Caesar; mark him.

CASSIUS
Casca, be sudden, for we fear prevention.
Brutus, what shall be done? If this be known,
Cassius or Caesar never shall turn back,
For I will slay myself.

BRUTUS
Cassius, be constant:
Popillius Lena speaks not of our purposes;
For, look, he smiles, and Caesar doth not change.

CASSIUS
Trebonius knows his time; for, look you, Brutus.
He draws Mark Antony out of the way.

[Exeunt ANTONY and TREBONIUS.]

DECIUS BRUTUS
    Where is Metellus Cimber? Let him go,
    And presently prefer his suit to Caesar.

[CAESAR sits.]

BRUTUS
    He is address'd: press near and second him.

CINNA
    Casca, you are the first that rears your hand.

[The Conspirators and Senators take their places.]

CAESAR
    Are we all ready? What is now amiss
    That Caesar and his senate must redress?

METELLUS CIMBER [Coming forward and kneeling.]
    Most high, most mighty, and most puissant Caesar,
    Metellus Cimber throws before thy seat
    An humble heart,—

CAESAR
    I must prevent thee, Cimber.
    These couchings and these lowly courtesies
    Might fire the blood of ordinary men,
    And turn pre-ordinance and first decree
    Into the law of children. Be not fond,
    To think that Caesar bears such rebel blood
    That will be thaw'd from the true quality
    With that which melteth fools; I mean, sweet words,
    Low-crooked court'sies and base spaniel-fawning.
    Thy brother by decree is banished:
    If thou dost bend and pray and fawn for him,
    I spurn thee like a cur out of my way.
    Know, Caesar doth not wrong, nor without cause
    Will he be satisfied.

METELLUS CIMBER
    Is there no voice more worthy than my own
    To sound more sweetly in great Caesar's ear
    For the repealing of my banish'd brother?

BRUTUS [Coming forward and kneeling.]
    I kiss thy hand, but not in flattery, Caesar;
    Desiring thee that Publius Cimber may
    Have an immediate freedom of repeal.

CAESAR
    What, Brutus!

CASSIUS [Coming forward and kneeling.]
    Pardon, Caesar; Caesar, pardon:
    As low as to thy foot doth Cassius fall,
    To beg enfranchisement for Publius Cimber.

CASSIUS
    I could be well moved, if I were as you:
    If I could pray to move, prayers would move me:
    But I am constant as the northern star,
    Of whose true-fix'd and resting quality
    There is no fellow in the firmament.
    The skies are painted with unnumber'd sparks,
    They are all fire and every one doth shine,
    But there's but one in all doth hold his place:
    So in the world; 'tis furnish'd well with men,
    And men are flesh and blood, and apprehensive;
    Yet in the number I do know but one
    That unassailable holds on his rank,
    Unshaked of motion: and that I am he,
    Let me a little show it, even in this;
    That I was constant Cimber should be banish'd,
    And constant do remain to keep him so.

CINNA [Coming forward and kneeling.]
    O Caesar,—

CAESAR
    Hence! Wilt thou lift up Olympus?

DECIUS BRUTUS [Coming forward with LIGARIUS and kneeling.]
    Great Caesar,—

CAESAR
    Doth not Brutus bootless kneel?

CASCA [Coming forward and kneeling.]
    Speak, hands for me!

    [CASCA first, then the other Conspirators and BRUTUS last stab CAESAR.]

CAESAR
    Et tu, Brute! Then fall, Caesar.

                    [Dies.]

CINNA
> Liberty! Freedom! Tyranny is dead!
> Run hence, proclaim, cry it about the streets.

CASSIUS
> Some to the common pulpits, and cry out
> 'Liberty, freedom, and enfranchisement!'

BRUTUS
> People and senators, be not affrighted;
> Fly not; stand stiff: ambition's debt is paid.

[Exeunt LEPIDUS, POPILLIUS, other Senators, ARTEMIDORUS, SOOTHSAYER, and Citizens.]

CASCA
> Go to the pulpit, Brutus.

DECIUS BRUTUS
> And Cassius too.

BRUTUS
> Where's Publius?

CINNA
> Here, quite confounded with this mutiny.

METELLUS CIMBER
> Stand fast together, lest some friend of Caesar's
> Should chance—

BRUTUS
> Talk not of standing. Publius, good cheer;
> There is no harm intended to your person,
> Nor to no Roman else: so tell them, Publius.

CASSIUS
> And leave us, Publius; lest that the people,
> Rushing on us, should do your age some mischief.

BRUTUS
> Do so: and let no man abide this deed,
> But we the doers.

[Exit PUBLIUS.]

[Re-enter TREBONIUS.]

CASSIUS
Where is Antony?

TREBONIUS
Fled to his house amazed:
Men, wives and children stare, cry out and run
As it were doomsday.

BRUTUS
Fates, we will know your pleasures:
That we shall die, we know; 'tis but the time
And drawing days out, that men stand upon.

CASSIUS
Why, he that cuts off twenty years of life
Cuts off so many years of fearing death.

BRUTUS
Grant that, and then is death a benefit:
So are we Caesar's friends, that have abridged
His time of fearing death. Stoop, Romans, stoop,
And let us bathe our hands in Caesar's blood
Up to the elbows, and besmear our swords:
Then walk we forth, even to the market-place,
And, waving our red weapons o'er our heads,
Let's all cry 'Peace, freedom and liberty!'

CASSIUS
Stoop, then, and wash.

[They smear their hands with CAESAR'S blood.]

How many ages hence
Shall this our lofty scene be acted over
In states unborn and accents yet unknown!

BRUTUS
How many times shall Caesar bleed in sport,
That now on Pompey's basis lies along
No worthier than the dust!

CASSIUS
So oft as that shall be,
So often shall the knot of us be call'd
The men that gave their country liberty.

DECIUS BRUTUS
    What, shall we forth?

CASSIUS
    Ay, every man away:
    Brutus shall lead; and we will grace his heels
    With the most boldest and best hearts of Rome.

                    [Enter a Servant.]

BRUTUS
    Soft! Who comes here? A friend of Antony's.

SERVANT [Kneeling and falling prostrate.]
    Thus, Brutus, did my master bid me kneel:
    Thus did Mark Antony bid me fall down;
    And, being prostrate, thus he bade me say:
    Brutus is noble, wise, valiant, and honest;
    Caesar was mighty, bold, royal, and loving:
    Say I love Brutus, and I honour him;
    Say I fear'd Caesar, honour'd him and loved him.
    If Brutus will vouchsafe that Antony
    May safely come to him, and be resolved
    How Caesar hath deserved to lie in death,
    Mark Antony shall not love Caesar dead
    So well as Brutus living; but will follow
    The fortunes and affairs of noble Brutus
    Thorough the hazards of this untrod state
    With all true faith. So says my master Antony.

BRUTUS
    Thy master is a wise and valiant Roman;
    I never thought him worse.
    Tell him, so please him come unto this place,
    He shall be satisfied; and, by my honour,
    Depart untouch'd.

SERVANT [Rising.]
    I'll fetch him presently.

                    [Exit.]

BRUTUS
    I know that we shall have him well to friend.

CASSIUS
        I wish we may: but yet have I a mind
        That fears him much; and my misgiving still
        Falls shrewdly to the purpose.

BRUTUS
        But here comes Antony.

[Re-enter ANTONY.]

        Welcome, Mark Antony.

ANTONY
        O mighty Caesar! Dost thou lie so low?
        Are all thy conquests, glories, triumphs, spoils,
        Shrunk to this little measure? Fare thee well.
        I know not, gentlemen, what you intend,
        Who else must be let blood, who else is rank:
        If I myself, there is no hour so fit
        As Caesar's death hour, nor no instrument
        Of half that worth as those your swords, made rich
        With the most noble blood of all this world.
        I do beseech ye, if you bear me hard,
        Now, whilst your purpled hands do reek and smoke,
        Fulfil your pleasure. Live a thousand years,
        I shall not find myself so apt to die:
        No place will please me so, no mean of death,
        As here by Caesar, and by you cut off,
        The choice and master spirits of this age.

BRUTUS
        O Antony, beg not your death of us.
        Though now we must appear bloody and cruel,
        As, by our hands and this our present act,
        You see we do, yet see you but our hands
        And this the bleeding business they have done:
        Our hearts you see not; they are pitiful;
        And pity to the general wrong of Rome—
        As fire drives out fire, so pity pity—
        Hath done this deed on Caesar. For your part,
        To you our swords have leaden points, Mark Antony:
        Our arms, in strength of malice, and our hearts
        Of brothers' temper, do receive you in
        With all kind love, good thoughts, and reverence.

CASSIUS
>Your voice shall be as strong as any man's
>In the disposing of new dignities.

BRUTUS
>Only be patient till we have appeased
>The multitude, beside themselves with fear,
>And then we will deliver you the cause,
>Why I, that did love Caesar when I struck him,
>Have thus proceeded.

ANTONY
>I doubt not of your wisdom.
>Let each man render me his bloody hand:

>[Shakes hands with the Conspirators.]

>First, Marcus Brutus, will I shake with you;
>Next, Caius Cassius, do I take your hand;
>Now, Decius Brutus, yours: now yours, Metellus;
>Yours, Cinna; and, my valiant Casca, yours;
>Though last, not last in love, yours, good Trebonius.
>Gentlemen all,—alas, what shall I say?
>My credit now stands on such slippery ground,
>That one of two bad ways you must conceit me,
>Either a coward or a flatterer.
>That I did love thee, Caesar, O, 'tis true:
>If then thy spirit look upon us now,
>Shall it not grieve thee dearer than thy death,
>To see thy Anthony making his peace,
>Shaking the bloody fingers of thy foes,
>Most noble! In the presence of thy corpse?
>Had I as many eyes as thou hast wounds,
>Weeping as fast as they stream forth thy blood,
>It would become me better than to close
>In terms of friendship with thine enemies.
>Pardon me, Julius! Here wast thou bay'd, brave hart;
>Here didst thou fall; and here thy hunters stand,
>Sign'd in thy spoil, and crimson'd in thy lethe.
>O world, thou wast the forest to this hart;
>And this, indeed, O world, the heart of thee.
>How like a deer, tricken by many princes,
>Dost thou here lie!

CASSIUS
>Mark Antony,—

ANTONY

    Pardon me, Caius Cassius:
    The enemies of Caesar shall say this;
    Then, in a friend, it is cold modesty.

CASSIUS

    I blame you not for praising Caesar so;
    But what compact mean you to have with us?
    Will you be prick'd in number of our friends;
    Or shall we on, and not depend on you?

ANTONY

    Therefore I took your hands, but was, indeed,
    Sway'd from the point, by looking down on Caesar.
    Friends am I with you all and love you all,
    Upon this hope, that you shall give me reasons
    Why and wherein Caesar was dangerous.

BRUTUS

    Or else were this a savage spectacle:
    Our reasons are so full of good regard
    That were you, Antony, the son of Caesar,
    You should be satisfied.

ANTONY

    That's all I seek:
    And am moreover suitor that I may
    Produce his body to the market-place;
    And in the pulpit, as becomes a friend,
    Speak in the order of his funeral.

BRUTUS

    You shall, Mark Antony.

CASSIUS

    Brutus, a word with you.
    [Aside to BRUTUS.] You know not what you do: do not consent
    That Antony speak in his funeral:
    Know you how much the people may be moved
    By that which he will utter?

BRUTUS [Aside to CASSIUS.]

    By your pardon;
    I will myself into the pulpit first,
    And show the reason of our Caesar's death:
    What Antony shall speak, I will protest
    He speaks by leave and by permission,
    And that we are contented Caesar shall

Have all true rites and lawful ceremonies.
It shall advantage more than do us wrong.

CASSIUS [Aside to BRUTUS.]
    I know not what may fall; I like it not.

BRUTUS
    Mark Antony, here, take you Caesar's body.
    You shall not in your funeral speech blame us,
    But speak all good you can devise of Caesar,
    And say you do't by our permission;
    Else shall you not have any hand at all
    About his funeral: and you shall speak
    In the same pulpit whereto I am going,
    After my speech is ended.

ANTONY
    Be it so.
    I do desire no more.

BRUTUS
    Prepare the body then, and follow us.

[Exeunt all but ANTONY.]

ANTONY
    O, pardon me, thou bleeding piece of earth,
    That I am meek and gentle with these butchers!
    Thou art the ruins of the noblest man
    That ever lived in the tide of times.
    Woe to the hand that shed this costly blood!
    Over thy wounds now do I prophesy,—
    Which, like dumb mouths, do ope their ruby lips,
    To beg the voice and utterance of my tongue—
    A curse shall light upon the limbs of men;
    Domestic fury and fierce civil strife
    Shall cumber all the parts of Italy;
    Blood and destruction shall be so in use
    And dreadful objects so familiar
    That mothers shall but smile when they behold
    Their infants quarter'd with the hands of war;
    All pity choked with custom of fell deeds:
    And Caesar's spirit, ranging for revenge,
    With Ate by his side come hot from hell,
    Shall in these confines with a monarch's voice
    Cry 'Havoc,' and let slip the dogs of war;
    That this foul deed shall smell above the earth
    With carrion men, groaning for burial.

[Enter a Servant.]

You serve Octavius Caesar, do you not?

SERVANT
I do, Mark Antony.

ANTONY
Caesar did write for him to come to Rome.

SERVANT
He did receive his letters, and is coming;
And bid me say to you by word of mouth—
[Seeing the body.] O Caesar!—

ANTONY
Thy heart is big, get thee apart and weep.
Passion, I see, is catching; for mine eyes,
Seeing those beads of sorrow stand in thine,
Began to water. Is thy master coming?

SERVANT
He lies to-night within seven leagues of Rome.

ANTONY
Post back with speed, and tell him what hath chanced:
Here is a mourning Rome, a dangerous Rome,
No Rome of safety for Octavius yet;
Hie hence, and tell him so. Yet, stay awhile;
Thou shalt not back till I have borne this corpse
Into the market-place: there shall I try
In my oration, how the people take
The cruel issue of these bloody men;
According to the which, thou shalt discourse
To young Octavius of the state of things.
Lend me your hand.

[Exeunt with CAESAR'S body.]

SCENE II. The Forum.

[Enter BRUTUS and CASSIUS, and a throng of Citizens.]

CITIZENS
We will be satisfied; let us be satisfied.

BRUTUS

Then follow me, and give me audience, friends.
[Aside to CASSIUS.] Cassius, go you into the other street,
And part the numbers.
[To the Citizens.] Those that will hear me speak, let 'em stay here;
Those that will follow Cassius, go with him;
And public reasons shall be rendered
Of Caesar's death.

FIRST CITIZEN

I will hear Brutus speak.

SECOND CITIZEN

I will hear Cassius; and compare their reasons,
When severally we hear them rendered.

[Exit CASSIUS, with some of the Citizens. BRUTUS goes into the pulpit.]

THIRD CITIZEN

The noble Brutus is ascended: silence!

BRUTUS

Be patient till the last.
Romans, countrymen, and lovers! hear me for my cause, and be silent, that
you may hear: believe me for mine honour, and have respect to mine
honour, that you may believe: censure me in your wisdom, and awake your
senses, that you may the better judge. If there be any in this assembly, any
dear friend of Caesar's, to him I say, that Brutus' love to Caesar was no less
than his. If then that friend demand why Brutus rose against Caesar, this is
my answer: —Not that I loved Caesar less, but that I loved Rome more.
Had you rather Caesar were living and die all slaves, than that Caesar were
dead, to live all free men? As Caesar loved me, I weep for him; as he was
fortunate, I rejoice at it; as he was valiant, I honour him: but, as he was
ambitious, I slew him. There is tears for his love; joy for his fortune; honour
for his valour; and death for his ambition. Who is here so base that would
be a bondman? If any, speak; for him have I offended. Who is here so rude
that would not be a Roman? If any, speak; for him have I offended. Who is
here so vile that will not love his country? If any, speak; for him have I
offended. I pause for a reply.

ALL THE CITIZENS

None, Brutus, none.

BRUTUS

Then none have I offended. I have done no more to Caesar than you shall
do to Brutus. The question of his death is enrolled in the Capitol; his glory

not extenuated, wherein he was worthy, nor his offences enforced, for which he suffered death.

[Enter ANTONY and others, with CAESAR'S body.]

Here comes his body, mourned by Mark Antony: who, though he had no hand in his death, shall receive the benefit of his dying, a place in the commonwealth; as which of you shall not? With this I depart,—that, as I slew my best lover for the good of Rome, I have the same dagger for myself, when it shall please my country to need my death.

ALL THE CITIZENS
    Live, Brutus! live, live!

FIRST CITIZEN
    Bring him with triumph home unto his house.

SECOND CITIZEN
    Give him a statue with his ancestors.

THIRD CITIZEN
    Let him be Caesar.

FOURTH CITIZEN
    Caesar's better parts
    Shall be crown'd in Brutus.

FIRST CITIZEN
    We'll bring him to his house
    With shouts and clamours.

BRUTUS
    My countrymen,—

SECOND CITIZEN
    Peace, silence! Brutus speaks.

FIRST CITIZEN
    Peace, ho!

BRUTUS
    Good countrymen, let me depart alone,
    And, for my sake, stay here with Antony:
    Do grace to Caesar's corpse, and grace his speech
    Tending to Caesar's glories; which Mark Antony,
    By our permission, is allow'd to make.
    I do entreat you, not a man depart,
    Save I alone, till Antony have spoke.

58

[Exit.]

FIRST CITIZEN
Stay, ho! and let us hear Mark Antony.

THIRD CITIZEN
Let him go up into the public chair;
We'll hear him. Noble Antony, go up.

ANTONY
For Brutus' sake, I am beholding to you.

[ANTONY goes into the pulpit.]

FOURTH CITIZEN
What does he say of Brutus?

THIRD CITIZEN
He says, for Brutus' sake,
He finds himself beholding to us all.

FOURTH CITIZEN
'Twere best he speak no harm of Brutus here.

FIRST CITIZEN
This Caesar was a tyrant.

THIRD CITIZEN
Nay, that's certain:
We are blest that Rome is rid of him.

SECOND CITIZEN
Peace! let us hear what Antony can say.

ANTONY
You gentle Romans,—

ALL THE CITIZENS
Peace, ho! let us hear him.

ANTONY
Friends, Romans, countrymen, lend me your ears;
I come to bury Caesar, not to praise him.
The evil that men do lives after them;
The good is oft interred with their bones;
So let it be with Caesar. The noble Brutus
Hath told you Caesar was ambitious:

If it were so, it was a grievous fault,
And grievously hath Caesar answer'd it.
Here, under leave of Brutus and the rest—
For Brutus is an honourable man;
So are they all, all honourable men—
Come I to speak in Caesar's funeral.
He was my friend, faithful and just to me:
But Brutus says he was ambitious;
And Brutus is an honourable man.
He hath brought many captives home to Rome
Whose ransoms did the general coffers fill:
Did this in Caesar seem ambitious?
When that the poor have cried, Caesar hath wept:
Ambition should be made of sterner stuff:
Yet Brutus says he was ambitious;
And Brutus is an honourable man.
You all did see that on the Lupercal
I thrice presented him a kingly crown,
Which he did thrice refuse: was this ambition?
Yet Brutus says he was ambitious;
And, sure, he is an honourable man.
I speak not to disprove what Brutus spoke,
But here I am to speak what I do know.
You all did love him once, not without cause:
What cause withholds you then, to mourn for him?
O judgment! thou art fled to brutish beasts,
And men have lost their reason.

[ANTONY weeps.]

Bear with me;
My heart is in the coffin there with Caesar,
And I must pause till it come back to me.

FIRST CITIZEN
    Methinks there is much reason in his sayings.

SECOND CITIZEN
    If thou consider rightly of the matter,
    Caesar has had great wrong.

THIRD CITIZEN
    Has he, masters?
    I fear there will a worse come in his place.

FOURTH CITIZEN
    Mark'd ye his words? He would not take the crown;
    Therefore 'tis certain he was not ambitious.

FIRST CITIZEN
If it be found so, some will dear abide it.

SECOND CITIZEN
Poor soul! his eyes are red as fire with weeping.

THIRD CITIZEN
There's not a nobler man in Rome than Antony.

FOURTH CITIZEN
Now mark him, he begins again to speak.

ANTONY
But yesterday the word of Caesar might
Have stood against the world; now lies he there.
And none so poor to do him reverence.
O masters, if I were disposed to stir
Your hearts and minds to mutiny and rage,
I should do Brutus wrong, and Cassius wrong,
Who, you all know, are honourable men:
I will not do them wrong; I rather choose
To wrong the dead, to wrong myself and you,
Than I will wrong such honourable men.
But here's a parchment with the seal of Caesar;
I found it in his closet, 'tis his will:
Let but the commons hear this testament—
Which, pardon me, I do not mean to read—
And they would go and kiss dead Caesar's wounds
And dip their napkins in his sacred blood,
Yea, beg a hair of him for memory,
And, dying, mention it within their wills,
Bequeathing it as a rich legacy
Unto their issue.

FOURTH CITIZEN
We'll hear the will: read it, Mark Antony.

ALL THE CITIZENS
The will, the will! we will hear Caesar's will.

ANTONY
Have patience, gentle friends, I must not read it;
It is not meet you know how Caesar loved you.
You are not wood, you are not stones, but men;
And, being men, bearing the will of Caesar,
It will inflame you, it will make you mad:
'Tis good you know not that you are his heirs;

For, if you should, O, what would come of it!

FOURTH CITIZEN
    Read the will; we'll hear it, Antony;
    You shall read us the will, Caesar's will.

ANTONY
    Will you be patient? will you stay awhile?
    I have o'ershot myself to tell you of it:
    I fear I wrong the honourable men
    Whose daggers have stabb'd Caesar; I do fear it.

FOURTH CITIZEN
    They were traitors: honourable men!

ALL THE CITIZENS
    The will! the testament!

SECOND CITIZEN
    They were villains, murderers: the will! read the will.

ANTONY
    You will compel me, then, to read the will?
    Then make a ring about the corpse of Caesar,
    And let me show you him that made the will.
    Shall I descend? and will you give me leave?

SEVERAL CITIZENS
    Come down.

SECOND CITIZEN
    Descend.

THIRD CITIZEN
    You shall have leave.

                    [ANTONY comes down.]

FOURTH CITIZEN
    A ring; stand round.

FIRST CITIZEN
    Stand from the hearse, stand from the body.

SECOND CITIZEN
    Room for Antony, most noble Antony.

                    [Enter ANTONY below.]

ANTONY
  Nay, press not so upon me; stand far off.

SEVERAL CITIZENS
  Stand back; room; bear back.

ANTONY
  If you have tears, prepare to shed them now.
  You all do know this mantle: I remember
  The first time ever Caesar put it on;
  'Twas on a summer's evening, in his tent,
  That day he overcame the Nervii:
  Look, in this place ran Cassius' dagger through:
  See what a rent the envious Casca made:
  Through this the well-beloved Brutus stabb'd;
  And as he pluck'd his cursed steel away,
  Mark how the blood of Caesar follow'd it,
  As rushing out of doors, to be resolved
  If Brutus so unkindly knock'd, or no;
  For Brutus, as you know, was Caesar's angel:
  Judge, O you gods, how dearly Caesar loved him!
  This was the most unkindest cut of all;
  For when the noble Caesar saw him stab,
  Ingratitude, more strong than traitors' arms,
  Quite vanquish'd him: then burst his mighty heart;
  And, in his mantle muffling up his face,
  Even at the base of Pompey's statue,
  Which all the while ran blood, great Caesar fell.
  O, what a fall was there, my countrymen!
  Then I, and you, and all of us fell down,
  Whilst bloody treason flourish'd over us.
  O, now you weep; and, I perceive, you feel
  The dint of pity: these are gracious drops.
  Kind souls, what, weep you when you but behold
  Our Caesar's vesture wounded? Look you here,
  Here is himself, marr'd, as you see, with traitors.

                    [ANTONY uncovers CAESAR'S body.]

FIRST CITIZEN
  O piteous spectacle!

SECOND CITIZEN
  O noble Caesar!

THIRD CITIZEN
  O woeful day!

FOURTH CITIZEN
O traitors, villains!

FIRST CITIZEN
O most bloody sight!

SECOND CITIZEN
We will be revenged.

ALL THE CITIZENS
Revenge! About! Seek! Burn! Fire! Kill! Slay!
Let not a traitor live!

ANTONY
Stay, countrymen.

FIRST CITIZEN
Peace there! hear the noble Antony.

SECOND CITIZEN
We'll hear him, we'll follow him, we'll die with him.

ANTONY
Good friends, sweet friends, let me not stir you up
To such a sudden flood of mutiny.
They that have done this deed are honourable:
What private griefs they have, alas, I know not,
That made them do it: they are wise and honourable,
And will, no doubt, with reasons answer you.
I come not, friends, to steal away your hearts:
I am no orator, as Brutus is;
But, as you know me all, a plain blunt man,
That love my friend; and that they know full well
That gave me public leave to speak of him:
For I have neither wit, nor words, nor worth,
Action, nor utterance, nor the power of speech,
To stir men's blood: I only speak right on;
I tell you that which you yourselves do know;
Show you sweet Caesar's wounds, poor poor dumb mouths,
And bid them speak for me: but were I Brutus,
And Brutus Antony, there were an Antony
Would ruffle up your spirits and put a tongue
In every wound of Caesar that should move
The stones of Rome to rise and mutiny.

ALL THE CITIZENS
We'll mutiny.

FIRST CITIZEN
    We'll burn the house of Brutus.

THIRD CITIZEN
    Away, then! come, seek the conspirators.

ANTONY
    Yet hear me, countrymen; yet hear me speak.

ALL THE CITIZENS
    Peace, ho! Hear Antony. Most noble Antony!

ANTONY
    Why, friends, you go to do you know not what:
    Wherein hath Caesar thus deserved your loves?
    Alas, you know not: I must tell you then:
    You have forgot the will I told you of.

ALL THE CITIZENS
    Most true. The will! Let's stay and hear the will.

ANTONY
    Here is the will, and under Caesar's seal.
    To every Roman citizen he gives,
    To every several man, seventy-five drachmas.

SECOND CITIZENS
    Most noble Caesar! We'll revenge his death.

THIRD CITIZEN
    O royal Caesar!

ANTONY
    Hear me with patience.

ALL THE CITIZENS
    Peace, ho!

ANTONY
    Moreover, he hath left you all his walks,
    His private arbours and new-planted orchards,
    On this side Tiber; he hath left them you,
    And to your heirs for ever, common pleasures,
    To walk abroad, and recreate yourselves.
    Here was a Caesar! when comes such another?

FIRST CITIZEN
    Never, never. Come, away, away!
    We'll burn his body in the holy place,
    And with the brands fire the traitors' houses.
    Take up the body.

SECOND CITIZEN
    Go fetch fire.

THIRD CITIZEN
    Pluck down benches.

FOURTH CITIZEN
    Pluck down forms, windows, any thing.

               [Exeunt Citizens with the body.]

ANTONY
    Now let it work. Mischief, thou art afoot,
    Take thou what course thou wilt!

                  [Enter a Servant.]

    How now, fellow!

SERVANT
    Sir, Octavius is already come to Rome.

ANTONY
    Where is he?

SERVANT
    He and Lepidus are at Caesar's house.

ANTONY
    And thither will I straight to visit him:
    He comes upon a wish. Fortune is merry,
    And in this mood will give us any thing.

SERVANT
    I heard him say, Brutus and Cassius
    Are rid like madmen through the gates of Rome.

ANTONY
    Belike they had some notice of the people,
    How I had moved them. Bring me to Octavius.

[Exeunt.]

SCENE III. A street.

[Enter CINNA the poet.]

CINNA THE POET
>I dreamt to-night that I did feast with Caesar,
>And things unlucky charge my fantasy:
>I have no will to wander forth of doors,
>Yet something leads me forth.

[Enter Citizens.]

FIRST CITIZEN
>What is your name?

SECOND CITIZEN
>Whither are you going?

THIRD CITIZEN
>Where do you dwell?

FOURTH CITIZEN
>Are you a married man or a bachelor?

SECOND CITIZEN
>Answer every man directly.

FIRST CITIZEN
>Ay, and briefly.

FOURTH CITIZEN
>Ay, and wisely.

THIRD CITIZEN
>Ay, and truly, you were best.

CINNA THE POET
>What is my name? Whither am I going? Where do I dwell? Am I a married man or a bachelor? Then, to answer every man directly and briefly, wisely and truly: wisely I say, I am a bachelor.

SECOND CITIZEN
>That's as much as to say, they are fools that marry: you'll bear me a bang for that, I fear. Proceed; directly.

CINNA THE POET
Directly, I am going to Caesar's funeral.

FIRST CITIZEN
As a friend or an enemy?

CINNA THE POET
As a friend.

SECOND CITIZEN
That matter is answered directly.

FOURTH CITIZEN
For your dwelling,—briefly.

CINNA THE POET
Briefly, I dwell by the Capitol.

THIRD CITIZEN
Your name, sir, truly.

CINNA THE POET
Truly, my name is Cinna.

FIRST CITIZEN
Tear him to pieces; he's a conspirator.

CINNA THE POET
I am Cinna the poet, I am Cinna the poet.

FOURTH CITIZEN
Tear him for his bad verses, tear him for his bad verses.

CINNA THE POET
I am not Cinna the conspirator.

FOURTH CITIZEN
It is no matter, his name's Cinna; pluck but his name out of his heart, and
turn him going.

THIRD CITIZEN
Tear him, tear him! Come, brands ho! fire-brands: to Brutus', to Cassius';
burn all: some to Decius' house, and some to Casca's; some to Ligarius':
away, go!

[Exeunt.]

ACT IV

SCENE I. A house in Rome.

[ANTONY, OCTAVIUS, and LEPIDUS, seated at a table.]

ANTONY
> These many, then, shall die; their names are prick'd.

OCTAVIUS
> Your brother too must die; consent you, Lepidus?

LEPIDUS
> I do consent—

OCTAVIUS
> Prick him down, Antony.

LEPIDUS
> Upon condition Publius shall not live,
> Who is your sister's son, Mark Antony.

ANTONY
> He shall not live; look, with a spot I damn him.
> But, Lepidus, go you to Caesar's house;
> Fetch the will hither, and we shall determine
> How to cut off some charge in legacies.

LEPIDUS
> What, shall I find you here?

OCTAVIUS
> Or here, or at the Capitol.

[Exit LEPIDUS.]

ANTONY
> This is a slight unmeritable man,
> Meet to be sent on errands: is it fit,
> The three-fold world divided, he should stand
> One of the three to share it?

OCTAVIUS
> So you thought him;
> And took his voice who should be prick'd to die,
> In our black sentence and proscription.

ANTONY

> Octavius, I have seen more days than you:
> And though we lay these honours on this man,
> To ease ourselves of divers slanderous loads,
> He shall but bear them as the ass bears gold,
> To groan and sweat under the business,
> Either led or driven, as we point the way;
> And having brought our treasure where we will,
> Then take we down his load, and turn him off,
> Like to the empty ass, to shake his ears,
> And graze in commons.

OCTAVIUS

> You may do your will;
> But he's a tried and valiant soldier.

ANTONY

> So is my horse, Octavius; and for that
> I do appoint him store of provender:
> It is a creature that I teach to fight,
> To wind, to stop, to run directly on,
> His corporal motion govern'd by my spirit.
> And, in some taste, is Lepidus but so;
> He must be taught and train'd and bid go forth;
> A barren-spirited fellow; one that feeds
> On objects, orts and imitations,
> Which, out of use and staled by other men,
> Begin his fashion: do not talk of him,
> But as a property. And now, Octavius,
> Listen great things:—Brutus and Cassius
> Are levying powers: we must straight make head:
> Therefore let our alliance be combined,
> Our best friends made, our means stretch'd
> And let us presently go sit in council,
> How covert matters may be best disclosed,
> And open perils surest answered.

OCTAVIUS

> Let us do so: for we are at the stake,
> And bay'd about with many enemies;
> And some that smile have in their hearts, I fear,
> Millions of mischiefs.

[Exeunt.]

SCENE II. Camp near Sardis. Before BRUTUS'S tent.

[Drum. Enter BRUTUS, LUCILLIUS, LUCIUS, and Soldiers; TITINIUS and
PINDARUS meeting them.]

BRUTUS
 Stand, ho!

LUCILLIUS
 Give the word, ho! and stand.

BRUTUS
 What now, Lucillius! is Cassius near?

LUCILLIUS
 He is at hand; and Pindarus is come
 To do you salutation from his master.

BRUTUS
 He greets me well. Your master, Pindarus,
 In his own change, or by ill officers,
 Hath given me some worthy cause to wish
 Things done, undone: but, if he be at hand,
 I shall be satisfied.

PINDARUS
 I do not doubt
 But that my noble master will appear
 Such as he is, full of regard and honour.

BRUTUS
 He is not doubted. A word, Lucillius;
 How he received you, let me be resolved.

LUCILLIUS
 With courtesy and with respect enough;
 But not with such familiar instances,
 Nor with such free and friendly conference,
 As he hath used of old.

BRUTUS
 Thou hast described
 A hot friend cooling: ever note, Lucillius,
 When love begins to sicken and decay,
 It useth an enforced ceremony.
 There are no tricks in plain and simple faith;
 But hollow men, like horses hot at hand,

Make gallant show and promise of their mettle;
But when they should endure the bloody spur,
They fall their crests, and, like deceitful jades,
Sink in the trial. Comes his army on?

LUCILLIUS
They mean this night in Sardis to be quarter'd;
The greater part, the horse in general,
Are come with Cassius.

BRUTUS
Hark! he is arrived.

[Low march within.]

[March gently on to meet him.]

[Enter CASSIUS and his powers.]

CASSIUS
Stand, ho!

BRUTUS
Stand, ho! Speak the word along.

FIRST SOLDIER
Stand!

SECOND SOLDIER
Stand!

THIRD SOLDIER
Stand!

CASSIUS
Most noble brother, you have done me wrong.

BRUTUS
Judge me, you gods! wrong I mine enemies?
And, if not so, how should I wrong a brother?

CASSIUS
Brutus, this sober form of yours hides wrongs;
And when you do them—

BRUTUS

    Cassius, be content.
    Speak your griefs softly: I do know you well.
    Before the eyes of both our armies here,
    Which should perceive nothing but love from us,
    Let us not wrangle: bid them move away;
    Then in my tent, Cassius, enlarge your griefs,
    And I will give you audience.

CASSIUS

    Pindarus,
    Bid our commanders lead their charges off
    A little from this ground.

BRUTUS

    Lucillius, do you the like; and let no man
    Come to our tent till we have done our conference.
    Let Lucius and Titinius guard our door.

[Exeunt.]

SCENE III. Brutus's tent.

[Enter BRUTUS and CASSIUS.]

CASSIUS

    That you have wrong'd me doth appear in this:
    You have condemn'd and noted Lucius Pella
    For taking bribes here of the Sardians;
    Wherein my letters, praying on his side,
    Because I knew the man, were slighted off.

BRUTUS

    You wronged yourself to write in such a case.

CASSIUS

    In such a time as this it is not meet
    That every nice offence should bear his comment.

BRUTUS

    Let me tell you, Cassius, you yourself
    Are much condemn'd to have an itching palm;
    To sell and mart your offices for gold
    To undeservers.

CASSIUS
I an itching palm!
You know that you are Brutus that speak this,
Or, by the gods, this speech were else your last.

BRUTUS
The name of Cassius honours this corruption,
And chastisement doth therefore hide his head.

CASSIUS
Chastisement!

BRUTUS
Remember March, the ides of March remember:
Did not great Julius bleed for justice' sake?
What villain touch'd his body, that did stab,
And not for justice? What, shall one of us
That struck the foremost man of all this world
But for supporting robbers, shall we now
Contaminate our fingers with base bribes,
And sell the mighty space of our large honours
For so much trash as may be grasped thus?
I had rather be a dog, and bay the moon,
Than such a Roman.

CASSIUS
Brutus, bay not me;
I'll not endure it: you forget yourself,
To hedge me in; I am a soldier, I,
Older in practise, abler than yourself
To make conditions.

BRUTUS
Go to; you are not, Cassius.

CASSIUS
I am.

BRUTUS
I say you are not.

CASSIUS
Urge me no more, I shall forget myself;
Have mind upon your health, tempt me no further.

BRUTUS
Away, slight man!

CASSIUS
Is't possible?

BRUTUS
Hear me, for I will speak.
Must I give way and room to your rash choler?
Shall I be frighted when a madman stares?

CASSIUS
O ye gods, ye gods! must I endure all this?

BRUTUS
All this! ay, more: fret till your proud heart break;
Go show your slaves how choleric you are,
And make your bondmen tremble. Must I budge?
Must I observe you? must I stand and crouch
Under your testy humour? By the gods
You shall digest the venom of your spleen,
Though it do split you; for, from this day forth,
I'll use you for my mirth, yea, for my laughter,
When you are waspish.

CASSIUS
Is it come to this?

BRUTUS
You say you are a better soldier:
Let it appear so; make your vaunting true,
And it shall please me well: for mine own part,
I shall be glad to learn of noble men.

CASSIUS
You wrong me every way; you wrong me, Brutus;
I said, an elder soldier, not a better:
Did I say 'better'?

BRUTUS
If you did, I care not.

CASSIUS
When Caesar lived, he durst not thus have moved me.

BRUTUS
Peace, peace! you durst not so have tempted him.

CASSIUS
I durst not!

BRUTUS
No.

CASSIUS
What, durst not tempt him!

BRUTUS
For your life you durst not!

CASSIUS
Do not presume too much upon my love;
I may do that I shall be sorry for.

BRUTUS
You have done that you should be sorry for.
There is no terror, Cassius, in your threats,
For I am arm'd so strong in honesty
That they pass by me as the idle wind,
Which I respect not. I did send to you
For certain sums of gold, which you denied me:
For I can raise no money by vile means:
By heaven, I had rather coin my heart,
And drop my blood for drachmas, than to wring
From the hard hands of peasants their vile trash
By any indirection: I did send
To you for gold to pay my legions,
Which you denied me: was that done like Cassius?
Should I have answer'd Caius Cassius so?
When Marcus Brutus grows so covetous,
To lock such rascal counters from his friends,
Be ready, gods, with all your thunderbolts;
Dash him to pieces!

CASSIUS
I denied you not.

BRUTUS
You did.

CASSIUS
I did not: he was but a fool that brought
My answer back. Brutus hath rived my heart:
A friend should bear his friend's infirmities,
But Brutus makes mine greater than they are.

BRUTUS
I do not, till you practise them on me.

CASSIUS

You love me not.

BRUTUS

I do not like your faults.

CASSIUS

A friendly eye could never see such faults.

BRUTUS

A flatterer's would not, though they do appear
As huge as high Olympus.

CASSIUS

Come, Antony, and young Octavius, come,
Revenge yourselves alone on Cassius,
For Cassius is aweary of the world;
Hated by one he loves; braved by his brother;
Cheque'd like a bondman; all his faults observed,
Set in a note-book, learn'd, and conn'd by rote,
To cast into my teeth. O, I could weep
My spirit from mine eyes! There is my dagger,
And here my naked breast; within, a heart
Dearer than Plutus' mine, richer than gold:
If that thou be'st a Roman, take it forth;
I, that denied thee gold, will give my heart:
Strike, as thou didst at Caesar; for, I know,
When thou didst hate him worst, thou lovedst him better
Than ever thou lovedst Cassius.

BRUTUS

Sheathe your dagger:
Be angry when you will, it shall have scope;
Do what you will, dishonour shall be humour.
O Cassius, you are yoked with a lamb
That carries anger as the flint bears fire;
Who, much enforced, shows a hasty spark,
And straight is cold again.

CASSIUS

Hath Cassius lived
To be but mirth and laughter to his Brutus,
When grief, and blood ill-temper'd, vexeth him?

BRUTUS

When I spoke that, I was ill-temper'd too.

CASSIUS
Do you confess so much? Give me your hand.

BRUTUS
And my heart too.

[They embrace.]

CASSIUS
O Brutus!

BRUTUS
What's the matter?

CASSIUS
Have not you love enough to bear with me,
When that rash humour which my mother gave me
Makes me forgetful?

BRUTUS
Yes, Cassius; and, from henceforth,
When you are over-earnest with your Brutus,
He'll think your mother chides, and leave you so.

POET
[Within.] Let me go in to see the generals;
There is some grudge between 'em, 'tis not meet
They be alone.

LUCILLIUS
[Within] You shall not come to them.

POET
[Within] Nothing but death shall stay me.

[Enter Poet, followed by LUCILLIUS, TITINIUS, and LUCIUS.]

CASSIUS
How now! what's the matter?

POET
For shame, you generals! what do you mean?
Love, and be friends, as two such men should be;
For I have seen more years, I'm sure, than ye.

CASSIUS
Ha, ha! how vilely doth this cynic rhyme!

BRUTUS [To the poet.]
> Get you hence, sirrah; saucy fellow, hence!

CASSIUS
> Bear with him, Brutus; 'tis his fashion.

BRUTUS
> I'll know his humour, when he knows his time:
> What should the wars do with these jigging fools?
> [To the poet.] Companion, hence!

CASSIUS [To the poet.]
> Away, away, be gone.

[Exit poet.]

BRUTUS
> Lucillius and Titinius, bid the commanders
> Prepare to lodge their companies to-night.

CASSIUS
> And come yourselves, and bring Messala with you
> Immediately to us.

[Exeunt LUCILLIUS and TITINIUS.]

BRUTUS
> Lucius, a bowl of wine!

[Exit LUCIUS.]

CASSIUS
> I did not think you could have been so angry.

BRUTUS
> O Cassius, I am sick of many griefs.

CASSIUS
> Of your philosophy you make no use,
> If you give place to accidental evils.

BRUTUS
> No man bears sorrow better. Portia is dead.

CASSIUS
> Ha! Portia!

BRUTUS
    She is dead.

CASSIUS
    How 'scaped I killing when I cross'd you so?
    O insupportable and touching loss!
    Upon what sickness?

BRUTUS
    Impatient of my absence,
    And grief that young Octavius with Mark Antony
    Have made themselves so strong:—for with her death
    That tidings came;—with this she fell distraught,
    And, her attendants absent, swallow'd fire.

CASSIUS
    And died so?

BRUTUS
    Even so.

CASSIUS
    O ye immortal gods!

[Re-enter LUCIUS, with wine and taper.]

BRUTUS
    Speak no more of her. Give me a bowl of wine.
    [To CASSIUS.] In this I bury all unkindness, Cassius.

[BRUTUS drinks.]

CASSIUS
    My heart is thirsty for that noble pledge.
    Fill, Lucius, till the wine o'erswell the cup;
    I cannot drink too much of Brutus' love.

[CASSIUS drinks.]

BRUTUS
    Come in, Titinius!

[Exit LUCIUS.]

[Re-enter TITINIUS, with MESSALA.]

Welcome, good Messala.

Now sit we close about this taper here,
And call in question our necessities.

CASSIUS [Aside.]
    Portia, art thou gone?

BRUTUS
    No more, I pray you.

[They sit.]

Messala, I have here received letters,
That young Octavius and Mark Antony
Come down upon us with a mighty power,
Bending their expedition toward Philippi.

MESSALA
    Myself have letters of the selfsame tenor.

BRUTUS
    With what addition?

MESSALA
    That by proscription and bills of outlawry,
    Octavius, Antony, and Lepidus,
    Have put to death an hundred senators.

BRUTUS
    Therein our letters do not well agree;
    Mine speak of seventy senators that died
    By their proscriptions, Cicero being one.

CASSIUS
    Cicero one!

MESSALA
    Cicero is dead,
    And by that order of proscription.
    [To BRUTUS.] Had you your letters from your wife, my lord?

BRUTUS
    No, Messala.

MESSALA
    Nor nothing in your letters writ of her?

BRUTUS
    Nothing, Messala.

MESSALA

That, methinks, is strange.

BRUTUS

Why ask you? Hear you aught of her in yours?

MESSALA

No, my lord.

BRUTUS

Now, as you are a Roman, tell me true.

MESSALA

Then like a Roman bear the truth I tell:
For certain she is dead, and by strange manner.

BRUTUS

Why, farewell, Portia. We must die, Messala:
With meditating that she must die once,
I have the patience to endure it now.

MESSALA

Even so great men great losses should endure.

CASSIUS

I have as much of this in art as you,
But yet my nature could not bear it so.

BRUTUS

Well, to our work alive. What do you think
Of marching to Philippi presently?

CASSIUS

I do not think it good.

BRUTUS

Your reason?

CASSIUS

This it is:
'Tis better that the enemy seek us:
So shall he waste his means, weary his soldiers,
Doing himself offence; whilst we, lying still,
Are full of rest, defense, and nimbleness.

BRUTUS

 Good reasons must, of force, give place to better.
 The people 'twixt Philippi and this ground
 Do stand but in a forced affection;
 For they have grudged us contribution:
 The enemy, marching along by them,
 By them shall make a fuller number up,
 Come on refresh'd, new-added, and encouraged;
 From which advantage shall we cut him off,
 If at Philippi we do face him there,
 These people at our back.

CASSIUS

 Hear me, good brother.

BRUTUS

 Under your pardon. You must note beside,
 That we have tried the utmost of our friends,
 Our legions are brim-full, our cause is ripe:
 The enemy increaseth every day;
 We, at the height, are ready to decline.
 There is a tide in the affairs of men,
 Which, taken at the flood, leads on to fortune;
 Omitted, all the voyage of their life
 Is bound in shallows and in miseries.
 On such a full sea are we now afloat;
 And we must take the current when it serves,
 Or lose our ventures.

CASSIUS

 Then, with your will, go on;
 We'll along ourselves, and meet them at Philippi.

BRUTUS

 The deep of night is crept upon our talk,
 And nature must obey necessity;
 Which we will niggard with a little rest.
 There is no more to say?

CASSIUS

 No more. Good night:
 Early to-morrow will we rise, and hence.

BRUTUS

 Lucius!

[Enter LUCIUS.]

My gown.

[Exit LUCIUS.]

Farewell, good Messala:
Good night, Titinius. Noble, noble Cassius,
Good night, and good repose.

CASSIUS
O my dear brother!
This was an ill beginning of the night:
Never come such division 'tween our souls!
Let it not, Brutus.

BRUTUS
Every thing is well.

CASSIUS
Good night, my lord.

BRUTUS
Good night, good brother.

TITINIUS and MESSALA
Good night, Lord Brutus.

BRUTUS
Farewell, every one.

[Exeunt all but BRUTUS.]

[Re-enter LUCIUS, with the gown.]

Give me the gown. Where is thy instrument?

LUCIUS
Here in the tent.

BRUTUS
What, thou speak'st drowsily?
Poor knave, I blame thee not; thou art o'er-watch'd.
Call Claudius and some other of my men:
I'll have them sleep on cushions in my tent.

LUCIUS
Varrus and Claudius!

[Enter VARRUS and CLAUDIUS.]

VARRUS
    Calls my lord?

BRUTUS
    I pray you, sirs, lie in my tent and sleep;
    It may be I shall raise you by and by
    On business to my brother Cassius.

VARRUS
    So please you, we will stand and watch your pleasure.

BRUTUS
    I will not have it so: lie down, good sirs;
    It may be I shall otherwise bethink me.
    Look, Lucius, here's the book I sought for so;
    I put it in the pocket of my gown.

[VARRUS and CLAUDIUS lie down.]

LUCIUS
    I was sure your lordship did not give it me.

BRUTUS
    Bear with me, good boy, I am much forgetful.
    Canst thou hold up thy heavy eyes awhile,
    And touch thy instrument a strain or two?

LUCIUS
    Ay, my lord, an't please you.

BRUTUS
    It does, my boy:
    I trouble thee too much, but thou art willing.

LUCIUS
    It is my duty, sir.

BRUTUS
    I should not urge thy duty past thy might;
    I know young bloods look for a time of rest.

LUCIUS
    I have slept, my lord, already.

BRUTUS
    It was well done; and thou shalt sleep again;
    I will not hold thee long: if I do live,
    I will be good to thee.

[Music, and a song.]

    This is a sleepy tune. O murderous slumber,
    Lay'st thou thy leaden mace upon my boy,
    That plays thee music? Gentle knave, good night;
    I will not do thee so much wrong to wake thee:
    If thou dost nod, thou break'st thy instrument;
    I'll take it from thee; and, good boy, good night.
    Let me see, let me see; is not the leaf turn'd down
    Where I left reading? Here it is, I think.

[Enter the Ghost of CAESAR.]

    How ill this taper burns! Ha! Who comes here?
    I think it is the weakness of mine eyes
    That shapes this monstrous apparition.
    It comes upon me. Art thou any thing?
    Art thou some god, some angel, or some devil,
    That makest my blood cold and my hair to stare?
    Speak to me what thou art.

GHOST
    Thy evil spirit, Brutus.

BRUTUS
    Why comest thou?

GHOST
    To tell thee thou shalt see me at Philippi.

BRUTUS
    Well; then I shall see thee again?

GHOST
    Ay, at Philippi.

BRUTUS
    Why, I will see thee at Philippi, then.

[Exit Ghost.]

    Now I have taken heart thou vanishest:

Ill spirit, I would hold more talk with thee.
Boy, Lucius! Varrus! Claudius! Sirs, awake! Claudius!

LUCIUS
The strings, my lord, are false.

BRUTUS
He thinks he still is at his instrument.
Lucius, awake!

LUCIUS
My lord?

BRUTUS
Didst thou dream, Lucius, that thou so criedst out?

LUCIUS
My lord, I do not know that I did cry.

BRUTUS
Yes, that thou didst: didst thou see any thing?

LUCIUS
Nothing, my lord.

BRUTUS
Sleep again, Lucius. Sirrah Claudius!
[To VARRUS.] Fellow thou, awake!

VARRUS
My lord?

CLAUDIUS
My lord?

BRUTUS
Why did you so cry out, sirs, in your sleep?

VARRUS and CLAUDIUS
Did we, my lord?

BRUTUS
Ay: saw you any thing?

VARRUS
No, my lord, I saw nothing.

CLAUDIUS
   Nor I, my lord.

BRUTUS
   Go and commend me to my brother Cassius;
   Bid him set on his powers betimes before,
   And we will follow.

VARRUS and CLAUDIUS
   It shall be done, my lord.

[Exeunt.]

ACT V

SCENE I. The plains of Philippi.

[Enter OCTAVIUS, ANTONY, and their army.]

OCTAVIUS
  Now, Antony, our hopes are answered:
  You said the enemy would not come down,
  But keep the hills and upper regions;
  It proves not so: their battles are at hand;
  They mean to warn us at Philippi here,
  Answering before we do demand of them.

ANTONY
  Tut, I am in their bosoms, and I know
  Wherefore they do it: they could be content
  To visit other places; and come down
  With fearful bravery, thinking by this face
  To fasten in our thoughts that they have courage;
  But 'tis not so.

[Enter a Messenger.]

MESSENGER
  Prepare you, generals:
  The enemy comes on in gallant show;
  Their bloody sign of battle is hung out,
  And something to be done immediately.

ANTONY
  Octavius, lead your battle softly on,
  Upon the left hand of the even field.

OCTAVIUS
  Upon the right hand I; keep thou the left.

ANTONY
  Why do you cross me in this exigent?

OCTAVIUS
  I do not cross you; but I will do so.

[March. Drum. Enter BRUTUS, CASSIUS, and their Army; LUCILLIUS, TITINIUS, MESSALA, and others.]

BRUTUS
They stand, and would have parley.

CASSIUS
Stand fast, Titinius: we must out and talk.

OCTAVIUS
Mark Antony, shall we give sign of battle?

ANTONY
No, Caesar, we will answer on their charge.
Make forth; the generals would have some words.

OCTAVIUS [To his army.]
Stir not until the signal.

[ANTONY and OCTAVIUS meet BRUTUS and CASSIUS.]

BRUTUS
Words before blows: is it so, countrymen?

OCTAVIUS
Not that we love words better, as you do.

BRUTUS
Good words are better than bad strokes, Octavius.

ANTONY
In your bad strokes, Brutus, you give good words:
Witness the hole you made in Caesar's heart,
Crying 'Long live! hail, Caesar!'

CASSIUS
Antony,
The posture of your blows are yet unknown;
But for your words, they rob the Hybla bees,
And leave them honeyless.

ANTONY
Not stingless too.

BRUTUS
O, yes, and soundless too;
For you have stol'n their buzzing, Antony,
And very wisely threat before you sting.

ANTONY

    Villains, you did not so, when your vile daggers
    Hack'd one another in the sides of Caesar:
    You show'd your teeth like apes, and fawn'd like hounds,
    And bow'd like bondmen, kissing Caesar's feet;
    Whilst damned Casca, like a cur, behind
    Struck Caesar on the neck. O you flatterers!

CASSIUS

    Flatterers! Now, Brutus, thank yourself:
    This tongue had not offended so to-day,
    If Cassius might have ruled.

OCTAVIUS

    Come, come, the cause: if arguing make us sweat,
    The proof of it will turn to redder drops. Look;

                         [OCTAVIUS draws his sword.]

    I draw a sword against conspirators;
    When think you that the sword goes up again?
    Never, till Caesar's three and thirty wounds
    Be well avenged; or till another Caesar
    Have added slaughter to the sword of traitors.

BRUTUS

    Caesar, thou canst not die by traitors' hands,
    Unless thou bring'st them with thee.

OCTAVIUS

    So I hope;
    I was not born to die on Brutus' sword.

BRUTUS

    O, if thou wert the noblest of thy strain,
    Young man, thou couldst not die more honourable.

CASSIUS

    A peevish schoolboy, worthless of such honour,
    Join'd with a masker and a reveller!

ANTONY

    Old Cassius still!

OCTAVIUS
    Come, Antony, away!
    Defiance, traitors, hurl we in your teeth:
    If you dare fight to-day, come to the field;
    If not, when you have stomachs.

          [Exeunt OCTAVIUS, ANTONY, and their army.]

CASSIUS
    Why, now, blow wind, swell billow and swim bark!
    The storm is up, and all is on the hazard.

BRUTUS
    Ho, Lucillius! hark, a word with you.

LUCILLIUS [Standing forth.]
    My lord?

          [BRUTUS and LUCILLIUS converse apart.]

CASSIUS
    Messala!

MESSALA [Standing forth.]
    What says my general?

CASSIUS
    Messala,
    This is my birth-day; as this very day
    Was Cassius born. Give me thy hand, Messala:
    Be thou my witness that against my will,
    As Pompey was, am I compell'd to set
    Upon one battle all our liberties.
    You know that I held Epicurus strong
    And his opinion: now I change my mind,
    And partly credit things that do presage.
    Coming from Sardis, on our former ensign
    Two mighty eagles fell, and there they perch'd,
    Gorging and feeding from our soldiers' hands;
    Who to Philippi here consorted us:
    This morning are they fled away and gone;
    And in their steads do ravens, crows and kites,
    Fly o'er our heads and downward look on us,
    As we were sickly prey: their shadows seem
    A canopy most fatal, under which
    Our army lies, ready to give up the ghost.

MESSALA

    Believe not so.

CASSIUS

    I but believe it partly;
    For I am fresh of spirit and resolved
    To meet all perils very constantly.

BRUTUS

    Even so, Lucillius.

CASSIUS [Joining BRUTUS.]

    Now, most noble Brutus,
    The gods to-day stand friendly, that we may,
    Lovers in peace, lead on our days to age!
    But since the affairs of men rest still incertain,
    Let's reason with the worst that may befall.
    If we do lose this battle, then is this
    The very last time we shall speak together:
    What are you then determined to do?

BRUTUS

    Even by the rule of that philosophy
    By which I did blame Cato for the death
    Which he did give himself, I know not how,
    But I do find it cowardly and vile,
    For fear of what might fall, so to prevent
    The time of life: arming myself with patience
    To stay the providence of some high powers
    That govern us below.

CASSIUS

    Then, if we lose this battle,
    You are contented to be led in triumph
    Thorough the streets of Rome?

BRUTUS

    No, Cassius, no: think not, thou noble Roman,
    That ever Brutus will go bound to Rome;
    He bears too great a mind. But this same day
    Must end that work the ides of March begun;
    And whether we shall meet again I know not.
    Therefore our everlasting farewell take:
    For ever, and for ever, farewell, Cassius!
    If we do meet again, why, we shall smile;
    If not, why then, this parting was well made.

CASSIUS
  For ever, and for ever, farewell, Brutus!
  If we do meet again, we'll smile indeed;
  If not, 'tis true this parting was well made.

BRUTUS
  Why, then, lead on. O, that a man might know
  The end of this day's business ere it come!
  But it sufficeth that the day will end,
  And then the end is known. Come, ho! away!

[Exeunt.]

SCENE II. The same. The field of battle.

[Alarum. Enter BRUTUS and MESSALA.]

BRUTUS
  Ride, ride, Messala, ride, and give these bills
  Unto the legions on the other side.

[Loud alarum.]

  Let them set on at once; for I perceive
  But cold demeanor in Octavius' wing,
  And sudden push gives them the overthrow.
  Ride, ride, Messala: let them all come down.

[Exeunt.]

SCENE III. Another part of the field.

[Alarums. Enter CASSIUS and TITINIUS.]

CASSIUS
  O, look, Titinius, look, the villains fly!
  Myself have to mine own turn'd enemy:
  This ensign here of mine was turning back;
  I slew the coward, and did take it from him.

TITINIUS
  O Cassius, Brutus gave the word too early;
  Who, having some advantage on Octavius,
  Took it too eagerly: his soldiers fell to spoil,
  Whilst we by Antony are all enclosed.

[Enter PINDARUS.]

PINDARUS
    Fly further off, my lord, fly further off;
    Mark Antony is in your tents, my lord
    Fly, therefore, noble Cassius, fly far off.

CASSIUS
    This hill is far enough. Look, look, Titinius;
    Are those my tents where I perceive the fire?

TITINIUS
    They are, my lord.

CASSIUS
    Titinius, if thou lovest me,
    Mount thou my horse, and hide thy spurs in him,
    Till he have brought thee up to yonder troops,
    And here again; that I may rest assured
    Whether yond troops are friend or enemy.

TITINIUS
    I will be here again, even with a thought.

                     [Exit.]

CASSIUS
    Go, Pindarus, get higher on that hill;
    My sight was ever thick; regard Titinius,
    And tell me what thou notest about the field.

            [PINDARUS ascends the hill.]

    This day I breathed first: time is come round,
    And where I did begin, there shall I end;
    My life is run his compass. Sirrah, what news?

PINDARUS [Above.]
    O my lord!

CASSIUS
    What news?

PINDARUS [Above.]
    Titinius is enclosed round about
    With horsemen, that make to him on the spur;
    Yet he spurs on. Now they are almost on him.
    Now, Titinius! Now some light. O, he lights too.
    He's ta'en.

[Shout from within.]

And, hark! they shout for joy.

CASSIUS
    Come down, behold no more.
    O, coward that I am, to live so long,
    To see my best friend ta'en before my face!

[PINDARUS descends and enters below.]

    Come hither, sirrah:
    In Parthia did I take thee prisoner;
    And then I swore thee, saving of thy life,
    That whatsoever I did bid thee do,
    Thou shouldst attempt it. Come now, keep thine oath;
    Now be a freeman: and with this good sword,
    That ran through Caesar's bowels, search this bosom.
    Stand not to answer: here, take thou the hilts;
    And, when my face is cover'd, as 'tis now,
    Guide thou the sword.

[PINDARUS stabs him.]

    Caesar, thou art revenged,
    Even with the sword that kill'd thee.

[Dies.]

PINDARUS
    So, I am free; yet would not so have been,
    Durst I have done my will. O Cassius,
    Far from this country Pindarus shall run,
    Where never Roman shall take note of him.

[Exit.]

[Re-enter TITINIUS with MESSALA.]

MESSALA
    It is but change, Titinius; for Octavius
    Is overthrown by noble Brutus' power,
    As Cassius' legions are by Antony.

TITINIUS
    These tidings will well comfort Cassius.

MESSALA
> Where did you leave him?

TITINIUS
> All disconsolate,
> With Pindarus his bondman, on this hill.

MESSALA
> Is not that he t hat lies upon the ground?

TITINIUS
> He lies not like the living. O my heart!

MESSALA
> Is not that he?

TITINIUS
> No, this was he, Messala,
> But Cassius is no more. O setting sun,
> As in thy red rays thou dost sink to-night,
> So in his red blood Cassius' day is set;
> The sun of Rome is set! Our day is gone;
> Clouds, dews, and dangers come; our deeds are done!
> Mistrust of my success hath done this deed.

MESSALA
> Mistrust of good success hath done this deed.
> O hateful error, melancholy's child,
> Why dost thou show to the apt thoughts of men
> The things that are not? O error, soon conceived,
> Thou never comest unto a happy birth,
> But kill'st the mother that engender'd thee!

TITINIUS
> What, Pindarus! where art thou, Pindarus?

MESSALA
> Seek him, Titinius, whilst I go to meet
> The noble Brutus, thrusting this report
> Into his ears; I may say, thrusting it;
> For piercing steel and darts envenomed
> Shall be as welcome to the ears of Brutus
> As tidings of this sight.

TITINIUS
> Hie you, Messala,
> And I will seek for Pindarus the while.

[Exit MESSALA.]

Why didst thou send me forth, brave Cassius?
Did I not meet thy friends? and did not they
Put on my brows this wreath of victory,
And bid me give it thee? Didst thou not hear their shouts?
Alas, thou hast misconstrued every thing!
But, hold thee, take this garland on thy brow;
Thy Brutus bid me give it thee, and I
Will do his bidding. Brutus, come apace,
And see how I regarded Caius Cassius.
By your leave, gods:—this is a Roman's part
Come, Cassius' sword, and find Titinius' heart.

[Kills himself.]

[Alarum. Re-enter MESSALA, with BRUTUS, CATO, STRATO, VOLUMNIUS, and LUCILLIUS.]

BRUTUS
Where, where, Messala, doth his body lie?

MESSALA
Lo, yonder, and Titinius mourning it.

BRUTUS
Titinius' face is upward.

CATO
He is slain.

BRUTUS
O Julius Caesar, thou art mighty yet!
Thy spirit walks abroad and turns our swords
In our own proper entrails.

[Low alarums.]

CATO
Brave Titinius!
Look, whether he have not crown'd dead Cassius!

BRUTUS
Are yet two Romans living such as these?
The last of all the Romans, fare thee well!
It is impossible that ever Rome
Should breed thy fellow. Friends, I owe more tears
To this dead man than you shall see me pay.

I shall find time, Cassius, I shall find time.
Come, therefore, and to Thasos send his body:
His funerals shall not be in our camp,
Lest it discomfort us. Lucillius, come;
And come, young Cato; let us to the field.
Labeo and Flavius, set our battles on:
'Tis three o'clock; and, Romans, yet ere night
We shall try fortune in a second fight.

[Exeunt.]

SCENE IV. Another part of the field.

[Alarum. Enter fighting, Soldiers of both armies; then BRUTUS, CATO, LUCILLIUS,
and others.]

BRUTUS
    Yet, countrymen, O, yet hold up your heads!

CATO
    What bastard doth not? Who will go with me?
    I will proclaim my name about the field:
    I am the son of Marcus Cato, ho!
    A foe to tyrants, and my country's friend;
    I am the son of Marcus Cato, ho!

BRUTUS
    And I am Brutus, Marcus Brutus, I;
    Brutus, my country's friend; know me for Brutus!

[Exit.]

[Enter Soldiers. Soldiers kill CATO.]

LUCILLIUS
    O young and noble Cato, art thou down?
    Why, now thou diest as bravely as Titinius;
    And mayst be honour'd, being Cato's son.

FIRST SOLDIER
    Yield, or thou diest.

LUCILLIUS
    Only I yield to die:
    There is so much that thou wilt kill me straight;

[Offering money.]

Kill Brutus, and be honour'd in his death.

FIRST SOLDIER
We must not. A noble prisoner!

SECOND SOLDIER
Room, ho! Tell Antony, Brutus is ta'en.

FIRST SOLDIER
I'll tell the news. Here comes the general.

[Enter ANTONY.]

[To ANTONY.] Brutus is ta'en, Brutus is ta'en, my lord.

ANTONY
Where is he?

LUCILLIUS
Safe, Antony; Brutus is safe enough:
I dare assure thee that no enemy
Shall ever take alive the noble Brutus:
The gods defend him from so great a shame!
When you do find him, or alive or dead,
He will be found like Brutus, like himself.

ANTONY [To First Soldier.]
This is not Brutus, friend; but, I assure you,
A prize no less in worth: keep this man safe;
Give him all kindness: I had rather have
Such men my friends than enemies. Go on,
And see whether Brutus be alive or dead;
And bring us word unto Octavius' tent
How every thing is chanced.

[Exeunt.]

SCENE V. Another part of the field.

[Enter BRUTUS, DARDANIUS, CLITUS, STRATO, and VOLUMNIUS.]

BRUTUS
Come, poor remains of friends, rest on this rock.

[BRUTUS sits. STRATO falls asleep.]

CLITUS
> Statillius show'd the torch-light, but, my lord,
> He came not back: he is or ta'en or slain.

BRUTUS
> Sit thee down, Clitus: slaying is the word;
> It is a deed in fashion. Hark thee, Clitus.

[Whispers.]

CLITUS
> What, I, my lord? No, not for all the world.

BRUTUS
> Peace then! no words.

CLITUS
> I'll rather kill myself.

BRUTUS
> Hark thee, Dardanius.

[Whispers.]

DARDANIUS
> Shall I do such a deed?

CLITUS
> O Dardanius!

DARDANIUS
> O Clitus!

CLITUS
> What ill request did Brutus make to thee?

DARDANIUS
> To kill him, Clitus. Look, he meditates.

CLITUS
> Now is that noble vessel full of grief,
> That it runs over even at his eyes.

BRUTUS
> Come hither, good Volumnius; list a word.

VOLUMNIUS
  What says my lord?

BRUTUS
  Why, this, Volumnius:
  The ghost of Caesar hath appear'd to me
  Two several times by night; at Sardis once,
  And, this last night, here in Philippi fields:
  I know my hour is come.

VOLUMNIUS
  Not so, my lord.

BRUTUS
  Nay, I am sure it is, Volumnius.
  Thou seest the world, Volumnius, how it goes;
  Our enemies have beat us to the pit:

[Low alarums.]

  It is more worthy to leap in ourselves,
  Than tarry till they push us. Good Volumnius,
  Thou know'st that we two went to school together:
  Even for that our love of old, I prithee,
  Hold thou my sword-hilts, whilst I run on it.

VOLUMNIUS
  That's not an office for a friend, my lord.

[Alarum still.]

CLITUS
  Fly, fly, my lord; there is no tarrying here.

BRUTUS
  Farewell to you; and you; and you, Volumnius.
  Strato, thou hast been all this while asleep;

[STRATO awakes.]

  Farewell to thee too, Strato. Countrymen,
  My heart doth joy that yet in all my life
  I found no man but he was true to me.
  I shall have glory by this losing day
  More than Octavius and Mark Antony
  By this vile conquest shall attain unto.
  So fare you well at once; for Brutus' tongue

Hath almost ended his life's history:
Night hangs upon mine eyes; my bones would rest,
That have but labour'd to attain this hour.

[Alarum. Cry within, 'Fly, fly, fly!']

CLITUS
Fly, my lord, fly.

BRUTUS
Hence! I will follow.

[Exeunt CLITUS, DARDANIUS, and VOLUMNIUS.]

I prithee, Strato, stay thou by thy lord:
Thou art a fellow of a good respect;
Thy life hath had some smatch of honour in it:
Hold then my sword, and turn away thy face,
While I do run upon it. Wilt thou, Strato?

STRATO
Give me your hand first. Fare you well, my lord.

BRUTUS
Farewell, good Strato.

[Runs on his sword.]

Caesar, now be still:
I kill'd not thee with half so good a will.

[Dies.]

[Alarum. Retreat. Enter OCTAVIUS, ANTONY, MESSALA, LUCILLIUS, and the
army.]

OCTAVIUS
What man is that?

MESSALA
My master's man. Strato, where is thy master?

STRATO
Free from the bondage you are in, Messala:
The conquerors can but make a fire of him;
For Brutus only overcame himself,
And no man else hath honour by his death.

LUCILLIUS
    So Brutus should be found. I thank thee, Brutus,
    That thou hast proved Lucillius' saying true.

OCTAVIUS
    All that served Brutus, I will entertain them.
    [To STRATO.] Fellow, wilt thou bestow thy time with me?

STRATO
    Ay, if Messala will prefer me to you.

OCTAVIUS
    Do so, good Messala.

MESSALA
    How died my master, Strato?

STRATO
    I held the sword, and he did run on it.

MESSALA
    Octavius, then take him to follow thee,
    That did the latest service to my master.

ANTONY
    This was the noblest Roman of them all:
    All the conspirators save only he
    Did that they did in envy of great Caesar;
    He only, in a general honest thought
    And common good to all, made one of them.
    His life was gentle, and the elements
    So mix'd in him that Nature might stand up
    And say to all the world 'This was a man!'

OCTAVIUS
    According to his virtue let us use him,
    With all respect and rites of burial.
    Within my tent his bones to-night shall lie,
    Most like a soldier, order'd honourably.
    So call the field to rest; and let's away,
    To part the glories of this happy day.

                [Exeunt.]

                THE END

LaVergne, TN USA
23 April 2010
180346LV00002B/74/A